OAKLEY

The Last 100 Years

A Century of Village Life

*To commemorate 100 years of the
Parish Council in the village*

Contents Page

Acknowledgements 4

Foreword by George Elkin, Chairman of the Parish Council 5

Preface 6

Sketch map of Oakley pre–1940 7

Oakley – The last 100 years

    Life in Oakley 100 years ago 8

    Oakley and Deane Parish Council 11

    A look at Oakley's schools 13

    Pulpits and prayer books: 100 years of Worship 19

    A walk back in time through old Oakley 25

    High days and holidays: notable events 69

    Camp fires and camaraderie: Oakley's youth organisations ... 79

    Sport, song and socials: leisure through the years ... 86

    Carts and carriages: transport through the century ... 97

    Local personalities 102

Prologue – A Future from the past 109

List of photographs 111

Acknowledgements

We would like to thank the people and organisations, too numerous to mention individually, who have so willingly given valuable information and have lent us their precious photographs. Our thanks also to those who have shared with us their memories of times gone by. This book could not have been written without you.

We would also like to thank those in the village and our colleagues on the Parish Council who have encouraged us in this venture, our Editor, Jackie Rathband and Designers, Peter Gibbons and Peter Lounton who have guided us through the maze of book publishing. A special thank you goes to our families – Ian, Neil and Hannah Warner and James Blackman – who have for the last eighteen months, had to endure our many hours of 'Oakley hundred yearing' in addition to our Parish Council commitments.

Ros Blackman and Sally Warner
August 1994

Every effort is made to ensure accuracy, but the publishers do not hold themselves responsible for any consequences that may arise from errors or omissions.
© *Oakley and Deane Parish Council 1994.*

All rights reserved. No part of this publication may be reproduced, stored in a retrieval system or transmitted in any form or by any means – electronic, mechanical, photocopying, recording or otherwise – unless the written permission of the publisher has been given beforehand.

Published by Oakley and Deane Parish Council, 17 Hunters Close, Oakley
Printed and bound by John Dollin Marketing Services Ltd. Plot 5, Evingar Trading Estate, Ardglen Road, Whitchurch, Hants RG28 7BB

ISBN No. 0 9524606 0 2

Foreword

By George Elkin
Chairman of The Parish Council

When I first saw the volume of photographs collected together to form the basis for this book I was struck by the spirit of friendliness and generosity with which the villagers of Oakley had entered into this project – a spirit that has endured throughout its interesting history.

Over 50 villagers have come forward to lend their photographs and other treasured possessions, many of which are family heirlooms. They also spent many evenings recounting the history and story behind the photographs to Ros Blackman and Sally Warner. It was a memorable time for all as each photograph recalled either part of their lives or those of their parents and grandparents.

Many photographs were of the societies which have flourished over the past 100 years. Some have come and gone but many have continued albeit with a changed name. New societies have been formed so that today, there are over 40 different organisations to which one can belong.

The picture of the 1927/28 Oakley Boys Football team can be compared with that of today. There is the obvious change in fashion with much shorter shorts and the commercialisation of the game with the introduction of sponsors names on shirts. Some things never change however, like the men of Oakley's desire to dress up in women's clothes in an effort to raise money for charity as at the event celebrating the Coronation of King George VI and Queen Elizabeth in 1937.

Without Ros Blackman and Sally Warner, this book, published to celebrate 100 years of Oakley Parish Council, would not have happened. They have spent untold hours in the evenings and at weekends gathering information, talking to villagers, and writing and preparing the book. On behalf of the Parish Council I would like to express our gratitude for all their hard work and congratulate them on producing a superb book that gives a fascinating insight in the life of a country village during the last 100 years.

G. F. Elkin
August 1994

Preface

As Oakley residents ourselves, we share a great pride and interest in the village. With our involvement with the Parish Council and our appointment as Governors of the local junior school we became aware that there was no easily accessible history of Oakley.

With this in mind and the approaching centenary of the Parish Council movement we thought that a fitting way to commemorate the occasion would be to produce a book recalling life in the village over the last 100 years.

We therefore set about collecting photographs and meeting those who had lived here for many years and those who had moved away from the village. We were extremely pleased by the response we received to our requests and our only regret is that we have not been able to use every photograph so kindly lent to us, or to record everyone's memories of Oakley before the modern development that changed the face of the village for ever.

We hope that, by our efforts, we have filled a gap and that within the ensuing pages there will be something of interest to long established residents and newcomers alike, as well as to the many visitors who regularly enjoy our village.

Ros Blackman and Sally Warner
August 1994

Oakley Pre-1940

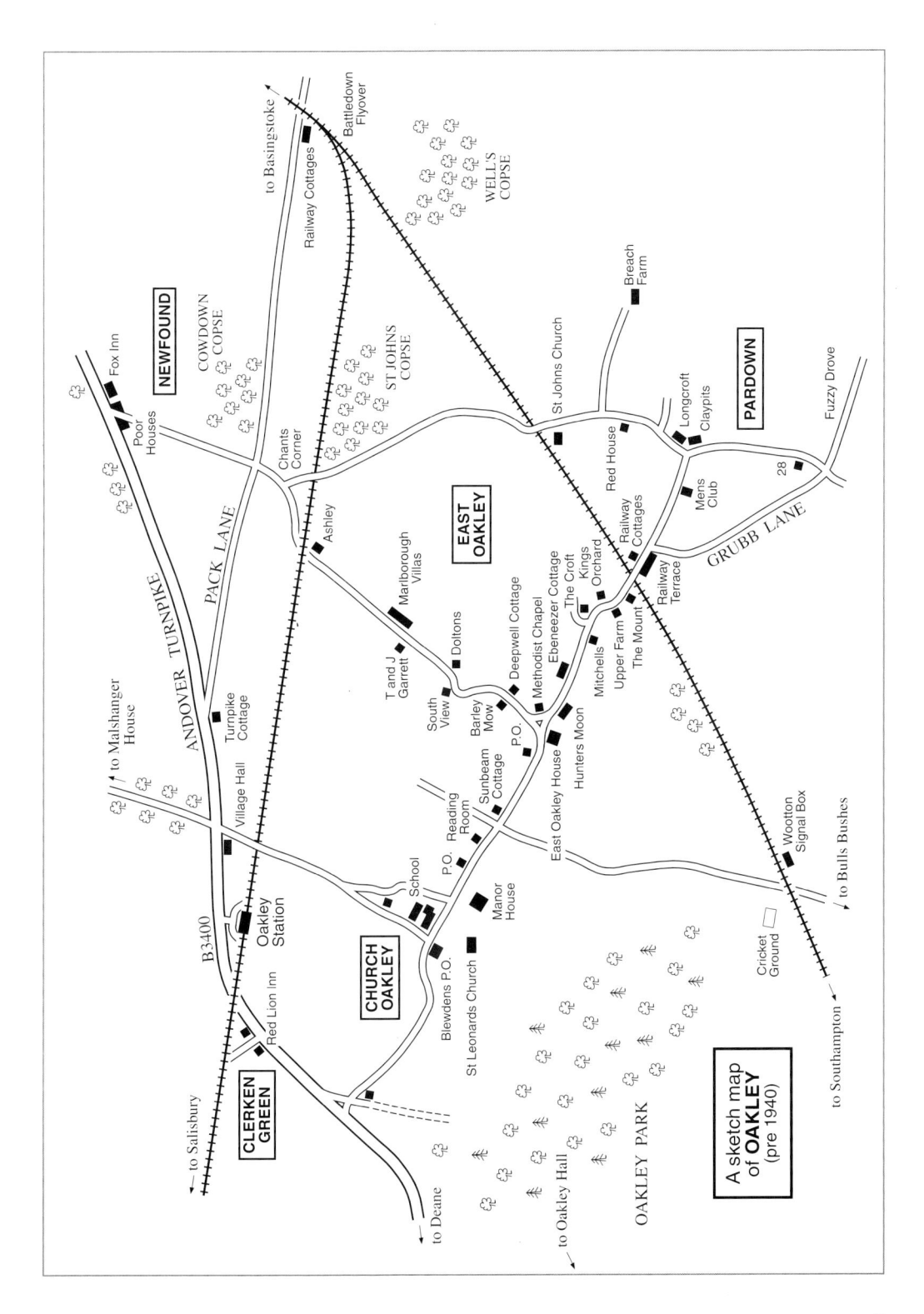

Life In Oakley 100 Years Ago

In the year 1894 when Queen Victoria was in the 57th year of her reign, William Gladstone was Prime Minister, Lyons Corner Tea Shops, Blackpool Tower and Tower Bridge were opened and Notts County won the FA Cup. Oakley was a small village with 810 inhabitants; 313 living in Church Oakley, 376 in East Oakley and Newfound and 121 at Deane. William Wither Bramston Beach, the Member of Parliament for the area until November 1885 owned Oakley Hall and a large proportion of Church Oakley. Wyndham Spencer Portal, papermaker and local JP, lived at Malshanger.

The village of Church Oakley centred around St Leonards Church, the cottages in Station Road and Rectory Road (referred to in the 1891 Census as Main Street). It encompassed Malshanger, White Lane, Clerken Green and south as far as Bulls Bushes. Deane was very much as it is today and included Oakley Hall and farm. East Oakley comprised the cottages around the pond and along Oakley Lane as far as the Barley Mow (in 1894 there were only or two cottages between Oakley Lane and Newfound), Hill Road, Claypits, and the single house in what is now St Johns Road called the Red House (now The Firs). At Newfound there were the cottages at the top of Fox Lane and on the Andover Turnpike (now B3400).

Most of the people living in the village were involved with agricultural work but the Census returns of 1891 mentions the following occupations – shoemaker, plumber, painter and glazier, railway employee, coachman, domestic servant, pondmaker, dressmaker, wheelwright, gamekeeper, carpenter, blacksmith, insurance agent, horse carter, policeman, roadman, well sinker and tea merchant.

Children attended the National School opposite the Church built in 1852/3 and extended in 1872 to accommodate 130 pupils. In 1894 there were approximately 116 pupils taught in two rooms. The Headmaster was George Figgins who was assisted by Miss Florence Rush (Pupil Teacher) and Miss Faires (Assistant Mistress). Mrs Caroline Beach the wife of the owner of Oakley Hall was a school manager.

In 1891 the School had begun operating under the 'Free Education' scheme – up until then pupils paid 1d/2d per week according to their circumstances. At this time school attendance was sporadic, interrupted as it was, by hay making, potato picking and beating. Outbreaks of mumps, ringworm, scarlet fever and diphtheria were responsible for yet more absences.

There was also an infant school at Deane (next to The Deane Gate) but the older children from the village walked to the school in Oakley. Pupils from East Oakley also attended the National School but those from Newfound were taught at Wootton St Lawrence.

There was little chance to travel and very few people went farther than Basingstoke. Trains were the main form of transport. They left from Oakley Station where James Fifield was Station–Master.

The social life of the village included concerts and magic lantern shows in the Reading Room in Rectory Road (on the site of the telephone exchange). There were four local 'alehouses', The Barley Mow where William Hunt was landlord, The Red Lion at Clerken Green (landlord William Few), The Fox Beer House (Emily Eckett) and the Deanegate (landlady Sarah Thwaites).

Oakley School early 1900s

Life In Oakley 100 Years Ago

St Leonards Church looking towards the West Door from the direction of the new Burial Ground soon after the yew trees were planted

As today, sports were a popular feature of village life. The cricket team played at Oakley Park, football was played in the field next to the Red Lion Inn and mention is made of skating on the pond in winter.

The main shops in 1894 were Blewdens next to the church who were grocer, baker and post office and a shop in Oakley Lane, run by Thomas Porter.

St Leonards Church had the Rev Hume as Rector with the Rev J Scott Ramsay listed as Curate. The Rector at Deane was Rev Gifford. St Johns Church had not been built by 1894 and many residents of East Oakley joined those from Newfound in walking to Wootton St Lawrence for services, often twice on Sundays.

Oakley And Deane Parish Council

In the Middle Ages as manor courts declined, the influence, wealth and responsibility of the Church increased. The parson was paid by means of a tithe which was a local income tax levied in kind on the produce of land. It is not surprising therefore that the inhabitants of a community began to meet together under the parson's direction for social and administrative purposes. Such meetings were often held in the vestry of the church after which they became known as Vestry Meetings

The Local Government Act 1894, which took a year to become enacted, excited much controversy particularly with the proposal to create parish councils. As a result the Church was to be excluded from formal participation in Local Government and the traditional functions of the parish were to be administered by laymen.

Thus, on the 14th December 1894, the first meeting of Oakley Parish Council (which did not include East Oakley, Pardown or Newfound) was held in the Parish Room. The members present at that meeting were James Balch a carpenter who lived in Station Road, James Fifield the Railway Station Master, Rev J Scott–Ramsay of Sunbeam Cottage, Job Oliver, farm labourer living in Station Road, Mrs Caroline Blewden, the Post Mistress. Mr William Wither Bramston Beach of Oakley Hall was elected Chairman. This appeared to be the only business conducted at that first meeting. More often than not in the early years there was little, or even no business, to transact at a Council meeting. Initially members of the Council were elected annually and meetings were held quarterly. Later, this changed to bi-monthly and now, apart from in August, meetings are held monthly.

The first village matter to which the Council gave their attention was the problem of roadside waste at Dell Farm. It was agreed that an enclosing fence be put up. Later, in 1895, it was agreed three lamps should be erected;, one near the post office, another by the pond and a third near the Parish Room. Walter Titcombe was appointed to look after the lamps for 2/6d (12.5p) per week during the period that they were required to be lit. To pay for this a rate of two pence in the pound was made.

As far back as 1896 the Council drew attention to the need for a recreation ground to be provided for the parish to celebrate Queen Victoria's long reign. It was suggested that it should be in the Glebe field.

Some other notable agenda items discussed during the last century include:

1917 Following a circular from Basingstoke Rural District Council, the Council was of the opinion that no extra houses for the working class were required for the Parish.

1926 Complaints made about irregular way of putting sharp flints down on the roads, unrolled and with no earth covering them.

Oakley And Deane Parish Council

1928 Discussions with Wootton Parish Council re: playing field for the village.

1935 Request made for fencing and danger lights at the pond opposite the Manor as two vehicles had recently been stranded there. Meeting requested with Chief Officer of Basingstoke Fire Brigade regarding the position for fixing the first fire hydrant.

1937 1d rate fixed to cover Parish Council expenses and a notice was sent to parishioners regarding an air raid precautions scheme organised by Sir J Colman, a parish councillor.

1948 Discussion re: inclusion of the Parish in the Borough of Basingstoke – objection made.

1952 The Clerk, Miss Edith Mabel Allen resigned after nearly 30 years of service.

1962 The Council inspected a map of the sewerage scheme for Church Oakley.

1965 Precept of £60.00. (£28,000 in 1994).

In 1966 a special Parish meeting was held to discuss the amalgamation of Church Oakley Parish Council and the East Oakley part of Wootton St Lawrence and a resolution was passed on 1st July 1966 to form one Parish Council. Elections were held in May 1968 and the first meeting of the new Council took place later that month. For the first time members from Church Oakley discussed planning applications.

In 1976 the Deane Parish Meeting was amalgamated with Oakley Parish Council bringing the total number of members to twelve. The name of the Council was then changed to include Deane.

Parish Council invoice from 1899 showing purchase of items for street lighting

A Look at Oakley's Schools

Education during the last one hundred years has changed in many ways not only nationally but also here in Oakley. The oldest recorded school was the 'Free' or 'Endowed' school erected during the lifetime of George Wither. Under his will a trust was created on 11th February 1667 to hold a house, garden and four acres of land and Gilbert Wither, his nephew, gave an annuity of £8 per annum, which was to provide for the education of eight poor children from the parishes of Church Oakley and Deane. The school was held in the building which originally stood on the site of the present Sunbeam Cottage in Rectory Road. It is not known exactly when the school ceased to exist but evidence shows that it was sometime between 1871 when it was last mentioned in the Hampshire Directory and 18th October 1877 when the premises were sold by the Trustees for £520.

At a later date Sunbeam Cottage became a cramming establishment for young gentlemen wishing to enter the Royal Military Academy at Sandhurst. Their tutor was Rev J Scott Ramsay who also took a great interest in the National School. The Old Malthouse was used as a dormitory. An advertisement for the school found in the 1895 edition of Kelly's Directory read as follows:

> Rev. J Scott Ramsay MA, assisted by three resident tutors of experience and high university standing, prepares a limited number of pupils for Army and University Examinations. Individual teaching and consequently marked success. References interchanged. A terms notice of removal required.
>
> Oakley is a small village 4 ½ miles from Basingstoke and 50 miles from London, situated in a really healthy and pretty district of North Hampshire. There is a billiard room on the premises and there are also three lawn tennis courts. In the Park there is a good cricket ground and a golf course. Railway Station and church near.

The National School is stated to have been built at the expense of Mr W Beach of Oakley Hall in 1852/53 for £450 and the premises now form part of St Leonards Centre. The building soon became too small and was extended in the 1870s by Mr William Wither Bramston Beach. A wooden classroom extension was constructed by Wyeths the Builders and was opened by Mr W G Hicks Beach on 15th September 1924.

The school had a meal scheme as long ago as 1910. Prominent people in the Parish used to supply fish and rabbits etc and parents took it in turns to cook the meals.

A Look At Oakley's Schools

Church Oakley School shortly after the construction of the wooden classroom in 1924

In 1933 the Oakley Hall Estate, which included the land, school and Headmaster's house, was sold. In 1934 the school was up for sale again and the Church Oakley Parochial Church Council decided to borrow £250 from the Diocesan Loan Fund to buy it and thus preserve it as a Church School.

Few changes were seen during the war years apart from the overflow of pupils created by the arrival of evacuees from Portsmouth and London being taught at what was then the new Andover Road Village Hall.

On 1st March 1950 Oakley School came under the control of Hampshire County Council but still retained its links with the Church. This action was forced upon the School Managers and the Parochial Church Council as they were unable to finance the cost of bringing the school up to the standards required by the Ministry of Education's building regulations.

Since 12th September 1949 children of eleven years upwards were attending Whitchurch Secondary Modern School (now known as Testbourne Community School). However, after considerable lobbying in the early 1960s, by the parents who felt that Oakley had greater ties with Basingstoke than with Andover, Hampshire County Council's Education Department eventually built Cranbourne School in Wessex Close. The majority of the children of that age group were transferred to the new school and continue to attend this and other Basingstoke schools today.

A Look At Oakley's Schools

The curriculum back in 1894 had, as could be expected, great stress laid on religious education. Visits to the school were made by the clergy three or four times a week to take prayers. In addition to what would now be regarded as religious education, the children were taught and regularly tested on the Lords Prayer, The Apostles Creed, The Ten Commandments, The Catechism and the Collects. Most of the time spent on secular education was taken up by reading, writing and arithmetic. Reference is made in the school Log Books to items of history and geography mainly learned by rote and learning school songs. Girls also had lessons in needlework, frequently using materials supplied by Mrs Caroline Beach, one of the School Managers and the wife of the owner of Oakley Hall, to whom the finished articles were returned.

Infant pupils of Oakley School in 1920
Back row: from left: Violet Fowle, Cathy Wootton, Agnes Marsh, Violet Dolton, Ted Allen, Winnie Ketch,
Second row: from left: (?), Evelyn Hunt, (?), Arthur Hopgood, Doris Chant, Kitty Smith
Third row: from left: Flo Pitman, Bertha West, Eileen Guy (? Gannon), Bill Moore, Jack Garrett, Basil Baston. Winnie Mullins
Fourth row: from left: Aileen Monger, (?), Bertha West (?), Gladys Neale, Nellie Saunders, Eunice Baston, (?).
Front row: from left: Monty Hunt, Arthur Dolton, Reg Whitbread, ? Bond, Tom Smith, (?), George Smith, Eric Morris
Teachers: Mr Bartram, Miss Blackburn, Miss Large (?), Mrs Dollin (?), Miss Kneller (?). There were three other assistants but it is not known which ones appear in the photograph.

A Look At Oakley's Schools

Although the 'National School' appears to have provided an education for the majority of children from Deane, Church Oakley and East Oakley. There was a school in Deane (on the corner of the Steventon road and the B3400) opened in April 1879 for the infants. Whilst there are no Log Books or documentary evidence, several references are made to children being transferred to and from an infants school in East Oakley. The children from Newfound attended school in Wootton St Lawrence and this continued until that school was closed on the opening of the Oakley Infant School in 1972. This was ten years after junior school children moved into new classrooms on the present site. During the period between 1962 and 1972, although geographically divided into two, educationally the schools were one, with one Headmaster – Mr Barrie Judge. Since 1972 the infants and juniors have been divided into two completely separate schools each with its own head teacher, staff and Board of Governors but there continues to be a close relationship between the two.

Older pupils of Oakley School in 1920
Back row: from left: (?), Fred Mullins, Percy Lush, (?), Arthur Eales, Bob Privett, Second row: from left: Betty Lee, Rose Speed, Winnie White, Irene Garrett, (?),
Third row: from left: Arthur Moore, (?), Jack Dollin, Clifford Chant, Archie Knight, Arthur Speed, Betty Phillis, Grace (?), Elsie Garrett, Bob Phillis, Nelson Kirby.
Front row: from left: Charlie Hunt, Mena Lee, Lilly Garrett, Mary Fuller, Reg Sims, Ray Sims, (?), Roy Kellow.

A Look At Oakley's Schools

It is interesting to note that, according to school records dating from 1863, the appointment of Miss Ann McDonald as head of the Junior School from 1st January 1995 will be the first time a woman has held this position since 1871. In that year the headmistress, one Miss Eliza Cox, left to marry George Webb, a yeoman of Summerdown and Ibworth.

Another school which existed for a short while in the 19th century was housed at the South View in Oakley Lane and was a private school for junior boarders.

Yet another school which has come and gone during the last 100 years is Hilsea College. The school was founded by John Ellis–Jones and opened its doors to its first pupils, – two boys on the 13th of January 1914 at Hilsea on the outskirts of Portsmouth. Between the wars it prospered and in 1930 moved to purpose–built buildings near Hilsea barracks. With the second world war becoming imminent the buildings were requisitioned by the Army in the late summer of 1939 and the school was given 24 hours to leave. Premises were found in Leigh Park at Havant but in 1940 these were requisitioned by the Navy and the school was on the move again, this time to Oakley Hall.

Oakley Hall – North front from the air

A Look At Oakley's Schools

Their arrival in Oakley was met with suspicion by the residents. Mr & Mrs Ellis–Jones, their three daughters, (one of whom married Mr Landon Platt and became co–principals) 2 teaching staff and the domestic staff from Portsmouth, together with forty boarders, were thought to be evacuees. On the first Sunday they attended St Leonards Church and were informed that Oakley Hall was in the Parish of Deane. From that day onwards the school built up a very close association with Deane, providing children for the choir and allowing the annual Church Fête to be held in the school grounds.

The school prospered at Oakley Hall, so much so that after the end of the war the property at Hilsea was sold and the Hilsea College remained in Oakley until it closed at the end of the summer term in 1992 when Mr & Mrs Platt retired.

Octagonal school room in grounds of Sunbeam Cottage

Pulpits & Prayer Books

100 Years Of Worship

Church and chapel have always been central to village life and Oakley, a century ago, was no exception. In 1894 there were four places of worship within the three parochial parishes – All Saints at Deane, St Leonards, Church Oakley, the Primitive Methodist Chapel in East Oakley and the Weslyan Methodist Chapel at Newfound. In 1913 work began on the fifth, St Johns Church, East Oakley.

St Leonards, Church Oakley is the oldest of the five buildings with parts dating back to the 12th century. Additions were made in the 15th and 16th centuries and it was substantially refurbished and added to in 1869. The architect for the later work, which included the addition of the vestry and the top part of the tower, was Mr Thomas H Wyatt and it was financed by the Portal family.

The clock on the tower and a tablet on the north inside wall of the tower were dedicated as a War memorial to the men of Church Oakley on September 7th, 1920. Other memorials to be found in the church today include the Psalm board, a tribute to Fred and Walter Titcombe and, on the wall behind the pulpit, a small crucifix hung in memory of Beatrice, first wife of Canon Jeudwine. The glass inner west door stands as a memorial to Marcus Lee.

Parish records began in May 1919 with the arrival of Canon Jeudwine and were recommenced in 1972 by Canon Litton. Some notable entries include:

13th April 1930 – the inauguration of a bus service to bring residents from White Lane, Malshanger and Summersdown to evensong.

1944 – resignation of Sexton, Mr L Sims after 38 years service.

1954 – organ overhauled at a cost of £117!

1979 – Miss Elsie Norman resigns the post of organist in 1979 after 37 years.

February 1978 – south aisle flooded after lead was stolen from the roof.

20th January 1980 – Mass was celebrated by Fr Brian Coogan (probably the first time since the Reformation).

The Rectors are appointed alternately by the Churchwardens and by the Provost and Fellows at The Queens College, Oxford. On Ascension Day of every year until October 1975, the Rectors had to pay a charge of 6/8d (33p) to the College.

Pulpits And Prayer Books: 100 Years Of Worship

All Saints Church, Deane was built on the site of the mediaeval Church of St Mary in 1818. It was designed in the Gothic style with sham windows in the tower which also houses five bells. The altar, pulpit and font are all modern.

Jane Austin's father was Rector of Deane from 1764 to 1801.

Christmas Day 1992 saw the beautiful new altar frontal being used for the first time, after many hours of work carried out by Mrs Jean Stanway a member of the Women's Institute at South Wonston, and an expert in Church Embroidery.

For many years until its closure in 1992, the boarders and staff from Hilsea College regularly attended Church at Deane and many of the children formed the choir.

All Saints Church, Deane

Pulpits And Prayer Books: 100 Years Of Worship

Parade outside the East Oakley Primitive Methodist Chapel

The land on which East Oakley Primitive Methodist Chapel was built, was owned by Mr Blackburn. He also owned the pair of cottages next door, (then known as Railway Croft but better known now as Alan's Folly, (see a walk back in time through old oakley). In March 1866 he agreed to sell the small plot for £5. Work on the building started immediately and the first service was held on 3rd June 1866 and by the autumn of that year the Sunday School officially started. Prior to the building of their Chapel, the Methodists of East Oakley had, for some considerable time, held their meetings in the pair of thatched cottages now known as Hunters Moon in Hill Road.

Records show that a branch of the Band of Hope had been set up by 1900 and several small children are shown as having taken the pledge.

The above picture shows an annual parade which took place in the summer and was known as a Camp Meeting or Hospital Sunday. The procession was led by either Basingstoke or Hannington Silver Band. The band would start by playing for about a quarter of an hour outside St Leonards Church and then proceed to march along Rectory Road towards the Primitive Methodist Chapel. A service was held outside the chapel before the band continued as far as Claypits returning for tea at Ebeneezer Cottage.

Pulpits And Prayer Books: 100 Years Of Worship

In 1944 the Chapel was extended by adding a room at the side with a sloping tin roof. It was built by a Mr Wyeth for the use of the Sunday School. By now electricity had been installed but there still was no water supply. A further modernisation programme was started in 1968, with voluntary labour, and it took 3 years to complete the installation of an electrical heating system, main drainage and a cold water supply. The kitchen has been extended and modernised several times, the latest being in 1991/92.

When the floor was replaced in 1981 a 'time capsule' was buried containing among other things – a membership list, service plan, financial statements, coins and bus tokens and a copy of the newspaper recording the wedding of the Prince of Wales and Lady Diana Spencer

Although the Chapel faced closure in 1965/66, when the membership dwindled to five, it is now once again flourishing with a church membership of nearly sixty.

The small Weslyan Methodist Chapel at Newfound was built in 1884 at a cost of less than £200. In the application, made in 1880, to erect the new chapel, it stated that the nearest place of worship to Newfound was the Parish Church, two miles away at Wootton and that the local population of 189 people were totally uncared for except for their own services held in a nearby cottage. The Primitive Methodist Chapel less than a mile away in East Oakley was ignored.

Weslyan Methodist Chapel, Newfound as it is in 1994 – a private residence

Pulpits And Prayer Books: 100 Years Of Worship

St Johns Church looking across the open space where St Johns Piece has now been built

By 1894 the building, fitted with coloured glass windows in the Weslyan fashion, needed modernising. The work, including plastering and colouring the inside walls, painting all woodwork, revarnishing matchboards and sundry repairs cost £12.3.6d. The Chapel was enlarged in 1905 by the addition of a vestry and classroom.

After 1932, when the Primitive and Weslyan Methodists merged, membership seemed to fall, and it was finally closed in 1986. The property was later sold and converted into an attractive private cottage retaining many of the chapel's original features.

St Johns Church, East Oakley is the newest of the five places of worship. Its foundation stone was laid on 11th September 1913, and it was built and furnished at the expense of Mr Sidney Bates to save the parishioners walking to Wootton St Lawrence to worship. It was designed by a Mr Hoyland and built of white cement stone by Messrs Blunden and Oliver of Basingstoke.

It is believed that the altar frontal was embroidered by some aunts in the Bates family who were accomplished needlewomen. Mrs Jean Stanway who more recently carried out work at All Saint's Church, Deane, undertook the task of repairing the embroideries in the early 1980s. The Communion Cup and Paten is a modern copy of the one at Wootton St Lawrence and was a gift from that Parish's vicar Rev Tapsfield.

The Church was consecrated on St John the Evangelist Day – 27th December 1914 by the Bishop of Winchester.

The War Memorial to the men of East Oakley who died in the first World War was unveiled by Lieutenant Colonel D S Bates and dedicated by the Rector on 12th December 1920.

The consecration of the Lychgate at the entrance to the churchyard took place on 14th November 1953. It was erected in commemoration of the Coronation of Queen Elizabeth II earlier in the year.

Church of England Children's Society: The collection boxes were first issued to members of Oakley Mother's Union in 1951. In April 1954, soon after her arrival in the village, Mrs Nancy Kirby was approached to take charge of the annual collection of the boxes and the counting of their contents. In that year eleven boxes produced £11.13.2 1/4d (£11.66). Forty years on, Mrs Kirby is still collecting the boxes. The total collected has increased over the years and in 1993 a grand sum of £2,160.69 was gathered from one hundred and twenty two boxes bringing the total for forty years to £20,933.82. Mrs Kirby can relate many interesting facts about the coins found in the boxes, such as six hundred and forty 'ship' half–pennies collected by one person in one year, another contributor put in only coppers (one old penny) bearing Queen Victoria's head.

A Walk Back in Time Through Old Oakley

We start our walk in the part of the village which is the most photographed and well known – The Pond at East Oakley at the junction of Oakley Lane, Rectory Road and Hill Road. Records show that there has been a pond on this site for nearly four centuries. During this period it has changed from the somewhat irregular and well used pond to the picturesque centre of the village that it is today. In the early part of this century the pond was used, as the photograph shows, to water livestock, not only horses but also cattle. Many older residents recall winter frolics, skating on the iced–over surface and building slides across it using lighted candles in jars for illumination.

Following the development of Oakley particularly the widening of Hill Road, it became a drainage pond for the surface water and silt. Along with the effects of the duck population, this led to the gradual silting up of the pond and the erosion of the banks, to such an extent that major renovation work was carried out between 1986 and 1989. Residents formed a Pond Preservation Committee and raised money for some of the improvements. The Scouts undertook the task of enlarging the island in the centre of the pond and one of the Cub Packs buried a 'time capsule' containing various items and information peculiar to the year 1986. After receiving advice from the Hampshire County Council officer with responsibility for Basingstoke Canal the work of draining the pond's 4,500 gallons of water and removing 21 tons of silt was carried out early in January 1989. Since then, renovation to the banks has been completed, aquatic plants are now thriving and the island is the proud possessor of a duck house.

Soldiers on horseback in the Pond – probably taken during the First World War

A Walk Back In Time Through Old Oakley

Hill Road Cottages on the left with Hunters Moon opposite. Photograph shows four cottages now converted into three, the first of which was the Police House

The first building on our walk is The Old Farmhouse in Hill Road. The first record of this property is on the Tithe Redemption Map of the area drawn up between 1841 and 1845 and it is believed to have been part of Follett's Farm.

Nearly opposite is 1, Hill Road which was at one time a Police House for the village policeman and is also more than 150 years old.

Hill Road has previously been known as Chapel Street and later Chapel Road

On the right, built with its frontage on the road, is Hunters Moon. Originally three cottages, part of the building is believed to be 300 to 350 years old and the rest approximately 150 years old. These were later converted into two and the property is now one family home. Before the building of the Primitive Methodist Chapel, one of the original three cottages was used as a meeting place for the congregation.

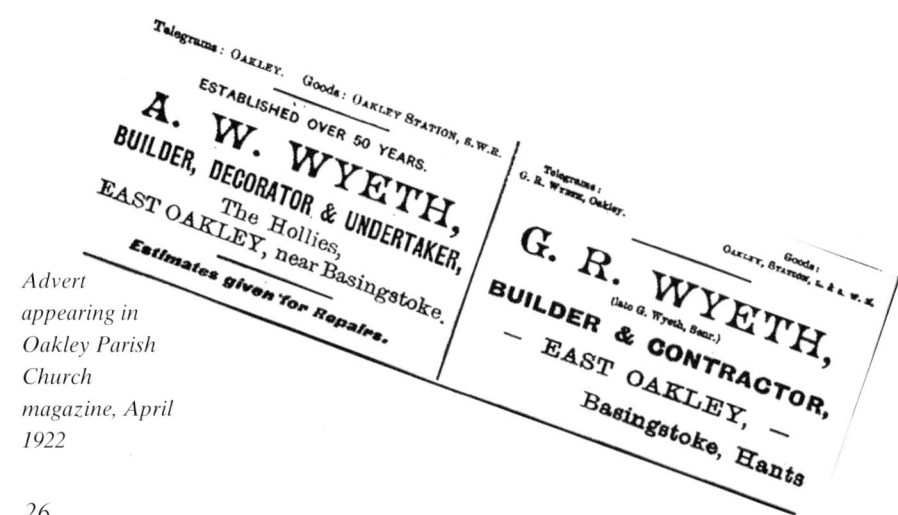

Advert appearing in Oakley Parish Church magazine, April 1922

Telegrams: OAKLEY.   Goods: OAKLEY STATION, S.W.R.

ESTABLISHED OVER 50 YEARS.

A. W. WYETH,
BUILDER, DECORATOR & UNDERTAKER,
The Hollies,
EAST OAKLEY, near Basingstoke.
Estimates given for Repairs.

Telegrams:
G. R. WYETH, Oakley.

OAKLEY, Goods,
STATION, L.&S.W.R.

G. R. WYETH,
(late G. Wyeth, Senr.)
BUILDER & CONTRACTOR,
EAST OAKLEY,
Basingstoke, Hants

A Walk Back In Time Through Old Oakley

Further along the road on the left is The Close which, with The Hollies and The Laurels were all built circa 1905. Before the construction of the houses in The Vale all the houses on the left–hand side of Hill Road had large plots of land on which orchards were planted and a variety of animals reared to feed the families. No.1, The Hollies had an air–raid shelter in the garden and the Home Guard also practised there. The Laurels' garden possessed a large barn from which Mr William Prentice distributed corn and chicken meal in small quantities to other smallholders in addition to rearing 2,000 to 3,000 head of poultry.

Between The Close and The Hollies is Ebeneezer Cottage which was constructed in 1899. This was owned by Mr Reg Wyeth whose father had helped to build the Primitive Methodist Chapel and who with his brothers were also builders. The single–story addition to the left–hand side of the cottage at one time housed a shop run by Reg Wyeth's wife Elizabeth from which she sold groceries, sweets and paraffin. The shop closed in the early 1930s.

Back a little way on the right–hand side of the road is the premises now occupied by Mr Drew, the local vet, but this narrow–fronted building was originally built for George Blewden as a butcher's shop. Mr Mullins who still lives in Hill Road can remember putting the roof on during the period he was employed by Wyeths. The shop was later owned by Mr and Mrs George Court and many older residents can still remember when Mr Albert Bunn was the village butcher making deliveries on a trade cycle as far away as Malshanger and Hannington. During this period orders would be taken for the 'Sunday Joint' to be delivered at the end of the week.

Ebeneezer Cottage showing Mrs Elizabeth Wyeth's Shop circa 1910

However, as customers had regular orders (ie beef one week, lamb the next etc) if someone forgot to put in their weekly order, Mr Bunn would still deliver the correct meat. To the right of the cottage, on the right-hand side of the vet's, a driveway can now be seen. This was once the land on which a cottage stood at right angles to the row still standing.

Following along the same side of the road leads to Mitchells, built in the 18th century, and clearly shown on the 1841 map of the village of East Oakley. At one time the parents of Arthur Hunt (who owned Doltons Garage from the 1950s onwards) lived there. It was also the early home of Dr Gallimore the village's first resident doctor. The stables once used by the horse he rode on his visits have now been converted into a garage.

The Croft, Hill Road. This was George Smith's coalyard for many years prior to its demolition in the 1960s

Continuing up Hill Road, which until the late 1960s was nothing more than an ordinary village lane, it leads to the junction with The Drive and Upper Farm Road. Before the development of Oakley this small area looked very different. On the left where The Drive joins Hill Road there was The Croft to the left-hand side of which for many years, until its demolition in the 1960s, was George Smith's Coalyard. It was also George Blewden's butcher shop prior to the building of the premises on the other side of the road.

A Walk Back In Time Through Old Oakley

Upper Farm in Hill Road

To the right of The Croft was a large house standing in a considerable amount of ground. The house was known as Kings Orchard and was occupied in the 1940s by the Misses Jukes, one of whom was a piano teacher. It was later owned by a Mr Watson and at some stage it is reputed to have been a small mink farm. A large part of the garden was sold in the 1960s to a self-build organisation who built the thirty-two houses known as Kings Orchard. On the right was another pond, smaller than the one outside the Primitive Methodist Chapel but serving the same purpose of collecting surface water.

On the right-hand side of Hill Road just past its junction with Upper Farm Road stood Upper Farm House and Upper Farm, later to be known as Westbrook Farm. This was a dairy farm and at the time the photograph was taken the farm was owned by Mr Thomas Dibben the grandfather of Mrs Cooper (previously of Oakley Post Office). When a child, living in Basingstoke, she would travel to Oakley on a charabanc to visit her grandfather

Sidney Wright was the next owner followed by Robert Westbrook (hence Westbrook Close). The penultimate owner, prior to demolition and the sale of the land, was Mrs Collidge who bred show ponies. The most famous was Oakley Bubbling Spring who went on to sire many ponies and the prefix 'Oakley' is still being used today.

The Mount, Hill Road, showing how narrow the road was before the development in the area

The Mount, Hill Road, now looks completely different to the cottage originally built on the site in 1903 by Mr Alan Montgomery who described himself as an artist. From the 1915 Kelly's Directory we know that Mr W H Hide, an insurance agent, lived at the cottage. The next family to make it their home were the Lee's (of cricketing fame) who had moved to Oakley in 1915 and first lived at The Close.

Beyond the railway bridge beside which a footbridge was constructed in 1974/75 are some pensioners' bungalows on the left. Prior to their construction this was the site of Railway Cottages. The two cottages were built in 1840 as homes for the railway signalmen working at Wootton Signal Box and were demolished in the mid 1950s at the same time as the signal box.

On the right is Railway Terrace built on what was known as Hog Pen Field. The only apparent connection with the Railway being that they were built adjacent to the track. The ten cottages were built in 1869 and it is believed that some of them were first owned by Richard Blackburn. Their water supply was by means of a well which is located beneath the present bus shelter. To the left of the terrace is Sainfoin Lane leading to Sunnymead and Water Ridges (named after Water Ridges Field) built as council houses in 1970.

A Walk Back In Time Through Old Oakley

Railway Cottages, Hill Road taken from the area of The Chalks

Railway Terrace, Hill Road circa 1905. Mrs Chivers and Mrs Brown (the mother and grandmother of Mrs Stickland of Fox Lane) are seen standing in the garden

The next area off Hill Road is St Johns Piece the building of which started at the St Johns Church end shortly after the Second World War. Mrs Wilson (who is still living in the same house), and her family, were the first to move into one of the newly built houses in 1948. This was considered to be palatial with electricity, running water and an inside toilet etc compared with her previous home at Battledown Cottages which had no such facilities.

Continuing up Hill Road the next turning on the right leads into a small development of old people's bungalows owned by Basingstoke and Deane Borough Council and known as Petersfield after Peter Gannon who was the previous landowner. The Warden Scheme set up by the Parish Council, is unique in Hampshire. In the late 1970s it was recognised by the Parish Council that many of the residents were old and frail and in need of a higher level of care than was currently available in the community. After many hours of negotiation, although not willing to actually run the scheme, Hampshire County Council agreed to finance the cost of the provision of a Warden to visit the residents once or twice a day according to their needs. Over the years, improvements have been made such as the linking of all the bungalows with a control centre in Basingstoke and the appointment of Deputy Wardens.

St Johns Piece taken from the St Johns Road end, just after completion in the early 1950s

Back on Hill Road there is a cottage on the right-hand side which has recently been converted from a shop known as Hill Road Stores. Research shows that it was opened in the 1950s by George Darke and in an advert in the first issue of '*Link*' in April 1961 it was then known as Colwell Stores and run by Mr F W Rolls.

Further along is East Oakley Village Hall, currently best known for its weekly jumble sales in aid of a variety of village and charitable organisations. Few people know its early history of which there is a certain amount of confusion. Some records show that it was built as an amenity for East Oakley by Mr Sidney Bates during World War I and leased to East Oakley Men's Club whereas others show that it was built in 1916 at the expense of Rev Tapsfield the vicar of Wootton St Lawrence.

During the period from 1921 to 1956 it was used mainly by the Men's Club and provided the hub of the social life of this part of the village. Various improvements were made during these years; the hall was lengthened, a permanent stage was erected and the installation of electricity in 1928 (previously petrol lamps were in use). In addition the entrance was moved from the front to the side, towards the rear of the building, where it still is.

By 1956 the Men's Club, the main users of the hall, had ceased to exist and therefore as there was then effectively no management committee the hall faced closure. A Public Meeting was held on 26th July 1956 at which it was decided that the Hall should be maintained as an amenity for East Oakley and that an appeal should be launched to raise funds for essential repairs. Within a few months a great deal of the work had been carried out by local residents providing voluntary labour. There was a Grand Social held on 3rd November 1956 to mark the re-opening of the now re-named East Oakley Village Hall.

During the next few years more money was raised and grants obtained to further improve the facilities at the hall. As the facilities improved lettings increased. Down the years it has been used as a Welfare Clinic (from August 1957), a mobile cinema in 1959, Girl Guides and Brownies, and the Registrar of Births and Deaths, (March 1960). For a period from 1948 it also housed the fortnightly Mobile County Library and even today a plaque on the wall recognises this.

Today it continues to be used for many village activities; Luncheon Club, Good Companions and St John's Ambulance, to name but a few.

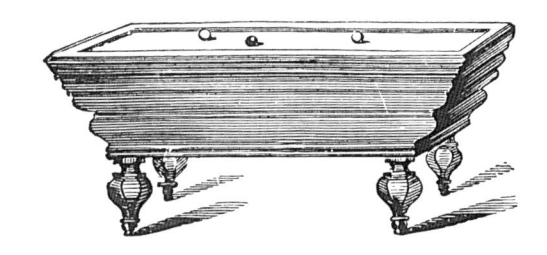

Peter Gannon (left) digging a new well at one of the first bungalows in Pardown circa 1912. With him are Robert and Emily Fowle on left of group. Modernised it is now the home of Mr and Mrs Baulch.

A short distance from the hall is the turning for Pardown on the right. Research shows that the first dwellings after those near the junction, were constructed from about 1910 onwards. These were tin bungalows with a water supply drawn from wells in the gardens.

There were about eight houses by the early 1930s and building slowly continued down the right-hand side of the whole length. At one time on the left of the road (further down from the Fuzzy Drove turning) there were copses and trees forming sunny glades, some of which became known as Strawberry Fields due to the abundance of wild strawberries in the summer. Unfortunately, with the need for more agricultural land these delights no longer exist.

Returning towards the junction, the entrance to Bakers of Oakley will be seen. The firm was first established in Pardown in the late 1950s but George Baker had arrived in Oakley some 20 years earlier. He started selling logs from a cart drawn by his horse, Bess, soon after the war. George's two eldest sons, Brian and Cyril, took over the log round in the early 1950s. However they could only make deliveries in the evenings and at weekends as, at the age of 13 and 12 they still attended school during the day.

By the late 1950s the brothers had bought their first lorry and in 1958 began to make deliveries of solid fuel. At that time they would collect this from Oakley Railway Station but later it came in by road service and they also commenced direct collection from pits in the Midlands. They soon purchased another lorry and then their brother Kenneth joined the business.

During the 1960s the business expanded rapidly and Bakers of Oakley began carrying general loads such as bricks for local housing and farm machinery for Perrys of Oakley. The latest branch of the business was started in anticipation of the opening of the M3 motorway – that of vehicle recovery specialists and the youngest brother David, started with the firm. This side of the business which provides a 24–hours, 365 days a year service continues to flourish. From their 'home–built' recovery vehicle, assembled from an ex–Army crane mounted on the redundant chassis from one of their lorries, the company has progressed to the recently purchased purpose–built heavy recovery unit.

Our next stop is at the junction called 'Claypits' believed to be named after the claypit which now forms part of the front garden of one of the nearby houses. The junction itself has only been in its present form for less than twenty years. Before the whole of Hill Road was widened there had been a grass triangle in the centre.

One of Bakers of Oakley's first coal lorries circa 1960, showing Cyril Baker loading coal

Longcroft with its barn is thought to be the oldest building still standing built by Wyeths. It is now a private residence but until the sale in 1919 it had been a dairy farm. James Wyeth also ran a building business from Longcroft.

A poster advertising the auction of Longcroft by Jennings & Lear at Claypits on Thursday 30th October 1919 at 12.30pm, a newspaper report of the event and other business documents are now in the care of the Willis Museum, Basingstoke. The advert lists that the following were among the items for sale: two active cart mares; eight dairy cows in milk; a four-wheeled van; a rick of meadow hay and two ricks of straw; various farm implements. The newspaper clipping reproduced below shows the way events were reported in great detail at that time.

> SALE OF FARM STOCK – Messrs Jenning & Lear conducted a successful sale of live and dead farm stock at Longcroft, Oakley on Thursday, the 30th ult., by instructions of Mr J Wyeth. The cows fetched good prices, making £48, £42.10s., £35, £34, £19, etc while the principal items of dead stock included Gower's corn and seed drill £25, Bamford's grass cutter £15, heavy flat roller £9.10s., potato plough £4, triangle barrel churn £4, dung cart £11, iron water cart £8, Deering's horse rake £5. A rick of hay made £65, a rick of straw £15 and a rick of pea haulm £9.10s.

During the Second World War Joan Garrett ran a general store at Claypits probably in what is now Mrs Kirby's garage.

The five cottages adjoining Longcroft were, at the time of the Tithe Redemption Map of 1841, owned by Mr James Wyeth, Thomas Garrett, and James Ballard. When they were put up for sale by auction on 1st October 1930 their reserve price was not reached and three of them were subsequently sold to Mr Goddard for £450 on 9th March 1932.

A Walk Back In Time Through Old Oakley

In the latter part of the 1920s Mr Lush, who had a newspaper delivery round, lived in one of the Claypit Cottages and one of his paper–boys was Mr Amos Batten who still lives in Oakley Lane. In those days the papers were collected from Oakley Railway Station, except on Sundays when the boys had to cycle into Basingstoke before starting the round. Mr Batten's round consisted of Pack Lane, Oakley Lane, Hill Road, Pardown, then to Deane before finishing at Steventon. He had to supply his own cycle, started work at 7.30 am (later than today's paper boys!) and finished at mid–day. Mr Batten recalls that most houses had papers delivered with the Daily Mail and Daily Mirror costing 1d and the Sunday editions 2d (less than 1p). The *Hants and Berks* (the fore–runner of *The Basingstoke Gazette*) was delivered on Saturdays and the money collected on Mondays.

Claypits – showing Longcroft and cottages with grass triangle in the centre of the junction

Turning right from Claypits into St Johns Road, or St Johns Lane as it was known for many years, The Firs will be found on the left-hand side. Originally known as The Red House when it was first built in the 1880s by Stephen Goddard, it stood in nearly four acres of land. Several generations of the Goddard family have lived in the house and the great-grandson of the builder still lives in the Basingstoke area. Matthew Goddard, the son of the builder, was a signalman at Worting Junction Box and had access to old railway sleepers. Out of which he used his skills to build a stable, pony trap house, pig sties and a large barn. The water was supplied to the house from a well near the back door and during the 1921 drought it was deepened to 120 ft thus ensuring it never ran dry again. Much of the land which had been used as a kitchen garden, orchard and paddock was subject to compulsory purchase in the 1940s by the Basingstoke Rural District Council for £128 and part of St Johns Piece and Goddards Firs was later built on it.

The Firs, St Johns Road, originally known as The Red House

Just before St Johns Church there is St Johns Youth Centre. This was built in 1970 on land leased from the Church. Local benefactors financed its building by way of interest free loans which were repaid from the proceeds of fund-raising activities in which many villagers both young and old took part. During the 1970s, Manydown Farms ploughed and seeded the land in front of the centre and further funds were raised to tarmac the road.

In the last twenty years various improvements have been made. The Youth Club has used the centre (except for one small break) since it was built. In 1973 the St Johns Playgroup opened its doors at the centre under the leadership of Mrs Rita Hoskins and many pre–school children have spent and continue to spend very happy mornings under her team's guidance.

Passing over the railway bridge and into St Johns Road there would have been few houses to be seen prior to the development of the area in the 1960s, the majority of the land having been used for chicken farming and nurseries. Past St Johns Copse on the right, which once covered a far larger area than now, to the railway and Brickbat Hill and Chants Corner, names no longer used today. Brickbat Hill became so named during the period when there was a small brickworks in the area and Chants Corner, the junction of St Johns Road and Oakley Lane after Mr H Chant, a County Court Bailiff, who had Court Cottage built on the corner in 1910.

Turning right a little way along on the left stands a brick–built bus shelter, originally constructed in 1961 at a cost of £54 and financed jointly by the Oakley & Deane Womens Institute and the Parish Council. It was replaced around about 1986. Some 1930s bungalows in Fox Lane have changed little since they were built by Messrs Butsey, Phillis and Stirtridge. No. 4 Fox Lane was first occupied by a Mr Nutley who lived there for fifty years. Dubious progress was made when the well, which also served his neighbours at No. 3, was fitted with a mechanical pump. It would take ten minutes of turning to bring up just one gallon of water!

The junction with the B3400, or the Andover Turnpike as it was known, is soon reached and also the hamlet of Newfoundland later, for some reason which we have been unable to discover, the name was shortened to Newfound. Before the 1950s there were a greater number of dwellings and, with a line of high trees standing behind the cottages stretching from Dell Farm nearly to Pilfurlong (as the junction with Wootton Lane was known), it must have looked quite different. The Pilfurlong junction is near to the furthermost extent of the Parish. Turning at this point to continue the walk the site of three small cottages, demolished in the 1950s, is on the right between the junction and Manydown Lodge. In the autumn when the field has been ploughed the exact site may be detected by the differing colour of the soil. The modern house at the entrance to the estate has replaced an original octagonal one.

A little farther on to the left is the original site of Mears Garage. Wallace Evelyn Mears, whose family was shown in the 1891 Census to have lived in one of the cottages nearby, started his business of motor and cycle engineer in 1926. His sister Mrs Maud Baldwin, ran a sweet and grocery shop in the adjoining property. Unfortunately, in 1929 a fire started in the two thatched cottages next door and spread to the garage destroying it and badly damaging Mrs Baldwin's shop.

A Walk Back In Time Through Old Oakley

Mr Mears then moved to the present site and another garage was built together with the two bungalows, the furthest one becoming Mrs Baldwin's shop. In 1932, Mr Mears was joined by his nephew Mr Ronald Merritt and they continued to work together until Mr Mears' death in 1960. The garage was sold to Mr Trussler in March 1961 who in 1970 leased and later sold it to Mr Greg Oliver. Mr Merritt continued on the staff until he retired after 32 years in the business. Within the last few years it has again been sold and the site developed and modernised by Wheeler and Ayland Limited.

Mrs Baldwin continued to run her shop, which became a Post Office in September 1934, with the help of her two daughters. Unfortunately her daughters died. Mrs Baldwin was broken hearted, and she herself died within a short time. After being closed for a year the property was sold to the Simpson family and subsequently in 1959 to Ted and Jill Edwards. With stricter rules introduced for security reasons, the Post Office section closed in 1993 and the present owners, Jean and Colin Brant, took over in January of this year.

W E Mears Motor Cycle Engineer, Newfound circa 1927. Wallace Mears is on the motor bicycle on the left. Mrs Baldwin's shop is on the right

A Walk Back In Time Through Old Oakley

A little further back along the road on the right between the Manydown entrance and what used to be the Weslyan Methodist Chapel there were a total of five small cottages and a pond. No. 5 is still standing today but the terrace of four (No's 7, 9, 11 and 13 Newfound) of which two were thatched and two were tiled were demolished in the late 1950s and the pond has disappeared. Each cottage was built of chalk and comprised: a main room, a small kitchen and two bedrooms. In the shed at the back there was a water tap connected to a well. Oil lamps were used for lighting and each cottage had a vegetable plot. Mr Binfield, the father of Mrs Stacey who has lived in one of the Fox Lane bungalows since it was built in 1935, lived at 13 Newfound for 76 years and only moved out when it was demolished in the 1950s.

On the opposite side of the road to the Chapel, where two comparatively new houses stand, was the site of the laundry for Manydown House which at one time was run by Mrs Haslett. To the left of Mears Garage can be seen a milestone and the site of Benhams Cottage built in 1789 and destroyed by fire in the early 1960s.

Old Poor House: five cottages standing at the top of Fox Lane

A Walk Back In Time Through Old Oakley

The junction at the Fox Inn was very much narrower and thatched cottages could be seen on both sides of Fox Lane. The five cottages on the left had been built as poor houses in 1800 by the owner of Manydown and Deputy Lord Lieutenant of Hampshire, Lovelace Bigg–Wither. They were constructed of chalk with a flint damp course and the rafters were fir trees. They consisted of two rooms with three steps down from the main room into the kitchen and again their water supply was from a well in the garden. They were demolished in 1957 and 1/2 Fox Lane built on the land.

The cottages closest to The Fox Inn contained three dwellings with a 120–ft well in the garden. This was recently unearthed by builders extending the Fox Inn. The last people to live in these cottages prior to demolition were Messrs Holmes, Throwan and Smallbone.

Little is known of the origins of the Fox Inn except that it has been a beer house throughout the last one hundred years and, more than likely for, many years prior to that, Mrs Eckett was the beer retailer in 1895.

Past the Fox Lane junction, Rose Cottage, built in 1868 and once known as Moore's Farm is on the left. The 18th–century Dell Farm a little way along on the right was the home of one of the first Parish Councillors, Mr Frederick Allen who served between March 1901 and May 1925. Opposite the farm was another pond.

The Fox, Newfound in 1911, showing the cottages at the junction of the Andover Turnpike and Fox Lane. Rose Cottage can be seen on the extreme right

Our next small detour is into Pack Lane, where in 1937 there were four council houses, (these are still standing set back on the left), four new bungalows built by Akehursts of Overton and ten to twelve tin bungalows. It is also known that asbestos bungalows had been constructed because, in 1955, Mrs Rea, a former Parish Council Chairman, her husband and eight children moved into one at 25 Pack Lane – the only house large enough for the whole family. It had ⅔rds of an acre of garden and a 90-ft frontage and was demolished shortly after Mrs Rea moved out in 1973. Mrs Cousins owned a confectionery and tobacco shop in approximately 1937 in premises where the entrance to Tollgate Close now is. This was later owned by Mr Dean and became the centre for a fish delivery service.

Returning to the B3400, Turnpike Cottage is on the left. Although much of its history is unknown it is believed to have been built in about 1640 as a toll house and many of the roof timbers of the original part of the cottage are just tree trunks sawn in half. The cottage is shown on the 1841 Tithe Redemption Map of Church Oakley and was at that time owned by the Trustees of the Andover Road Turnpike and occupied by James Crouch. It was subsequently owned by Hampshire County Council as a roadman's cottage.

The recently refurbished brick–built bus shelter on the far side of Andover Road was erected in 1954 as the Parish Council's memorial of the Coronation of Queen Elizabeth II. Lady Colman presented a suitably – inscribed oak plaque which was fixed inside.

Looking slightly left across the field behind the bus shelter, is an avenue of lime trees planted along Malshanger Lane by the late Sir Wyndham Portal probably at the end of the last century. They still look beautiful on frosty winter mornings against the backdrop of a clear blue sky. The lane leads to the lodge on the corner at the bottom of the hill which marks the entrance to Malshanger House.

The original Tudor Manor House was believed to have been built in the 15th century but all that now remains is one lofty octagonal–shaped gate tower. It was at that time occupied by the Warham family, the most famous member being William Warham who held many high offices of state, among them Chancellor of England, and for the last 28 years of his life until his death in 1532, that of Archbishop of Canterbury.

The existing house was built at the beginning of the last century by the first Lord Thurlow who was Lord Chancellor and in approximately 1858 the property was purchased by Sir Wyndham Portal. It remained in that family's ownership for 50 years. Sir Wyndham and Lady Portal celebrated their golden wedding on 19th April 1899 which the comparatively new Parish Council marked by presenting them with the gift of a silver casket enclosing a suitably inscribed scroll.

Malshanger House circa 1909

It is interesting to note that on the night of the Census on 18th April 1891 there were fifteen family members in residence at Malshanger together with five lady's maids, three nurses, four housemaids, one kitchenmaid, one scullerymaid, three footmen, one groom and one stable helper.

When the Portal family sold the estate it had two other owners, Mr Godfrey Walter, at one point the owner of The Times newspaper and Sir Hill Child, Comptroller of the Kings Household before it was acquired by the Colman family in 1934.

During the first five years of their ownership many improvements were made not only to the house and gardens but also to the surrounding farms. The most important improvements were that the well at Sheardown House was deepened to allow water to be pumped all over the estate and electricity was installed in all the buildings.

A Walk Back In Time Through Old Oakley

The outbreak of the Second World War saw further changes with Malshanger being used for families evacuated from Portsmouth and expectant mothers from London. It also became a resident nursery for under–fives whose mothers stayed in Portsmouth to look after their menfolk.

The early 1940s saw the billeting of a Bomb Disposal Unit at the house which also became a WVS centre and clothing store and the grounds were used by the Home Guard and the Civil Defence for training and exercises.

Part of the house was demolished in 1955 to make it a more manageable size for the younger generation. It still remains in the ownership of the Colman family with Sir Michael and Lady Colman residing in part, the rest being used by the Warham Trust.

Returning to the cross roads of Andover Road, Malshanger Lane and Station Road, the Andover Road Village Hall can be seen on the right a few yards into Station Road. The Hall, a gift to Church Oakley, Deane, East Oakley, Malshanger and Newfound from Mr Jeremiah Colman (he became Sir Jeremiah during World War II) was officially opened on May 19th 1938. Although due to the large increase in the population, it cannot stage the kind of village social events it has in the past, many organisations still regularly use the facility.

Back onto the Andover Turnpike a left turn under the railway bridge leads to Clerken Green with the sites of Oakley Coaches and the Beach Arms Hotel on the right. Oakley Coaches, with their mainly red and yellow painted coaches started in business in 1970. The company are well known in Oakley and the surrounding villages by the older school children for the double–decker school buses especially the one painted pink and affectionately known as 'The Pink Panther'. The owner Michael Jones, bought his first coach, a 1964 Bedford Plaxton in 1970 and the fleet of vehicles grew until late in 1985 when the present site was purchased.

Prior to this the site was the home of the Beach Arms Service Station. The petrol station was originally built in about 1928 by Mr William Guy Hicks Beach and was shortly afterwards described by the Minister for Transport as 'an Ideal Filling Station'. In 1931 both The Beach Arms and the filling station were sold to John Davenport and Sons Brewery Limited. (This sale, together with The Deane Gate Inn raised £16,200).

Beach Arms Service Station in 1963, showing their accident recovery truck

They extended the garage site intending to run a bottling depot there, however, when this failed to mature the whole site was sold to Friary Brewery of Guildford. In 1938 Mr Harold Seeney bought the filling station and built the adjoining house. In addition to the filling station Mr Seeney carried out tractor repairs and later charged radio accumulators. (Customers used to have three accumulators, one in use, one being charged and one awaiting collection).

45

A Walk Back In Time Through Old Oakley

In its heyday, when the road was still the main route to and from the West Country, the garage carried out repairs (mainly for customers in Church Oakley, Hannington and Ibworth), had a car show room, a kiosk where tobacco, sweets and car parts were sold and an accident recovery vehicle.

Across Ivydown Lane now stands the mock–Tudor–looking Beach Arms Hotel, built in 1801 and originally known as the Red Lion Inn. The Tithe Redemption map of 1841 shows a house on the site owned by William Beach and occupied by Hannah Allen. The first reference to the property being the Red Lion Inn is in *Whites Gazetteer of Hampshire* dated 1859 when Thomas Phillips was in occupation. By the time of the 1891 Census William Few was described as the Licensed Victualler. During the First World War annual cattle sales were held in the yard which was edged by a duck pond.

In 1926/27 Mr W G Hicks–Beach spent £6,000 on extensive alterations to turn it into the mock–Tudor–style it retains today. When the alterations were complete he renamed it the Beach Arms.

The Second World War saw concrete tank blocks stored on the forecourt of the Beach Arms. Depressions for these blocks were dug in the road and it was one of the duties of the Home Guard to move the blocks into the holes if Oakley or the surrounding district was invaded.

Red Lion Inn, Clerken Green in the late 1920s, prior to alterations, after which it was renamed

A Walk Back In Time Through Old Oakley

Following the war the Beach Arms was one of the stopping places for the Royal Blue Coaches on their journey between London, Exeter and the West Country and there was a cafeteria in the car park in which their customers could partake of refreshments served on the coach company's own monogrammed china.

Travelling westwards along the B3400 we pass the site of two more ponds, Spring Pond near East Lodge, Oakley Hall and Shepherds Pond on the right of the road. Until 1960 when various factors altered the water levels and drainage, the water table would rise approximately every 7 years and firstly the water level in Spring Pond would rise and flood the road. The water would flow into a culvert and then into Shepherds Pond. Some years the flooding was very bad and the whole area as far as the path to Deane Church would become flooded.

Floods at Deane – note temporary footbridge

47

A Walk Back In Time Through Old Oakley

The Rectory, Deane (now Deane Hill House). Built c.1850 to replace the original Rectory which was situated opposite the Church. The last Rector to live in the village was the Rev. Marle who retired in 1966.

A turning on the right leads into the village of Deane which has changed very little over the years. The 1891 Census shows that there were 47 males and 74 females living in 32 houses compared to the one taken one hundred years later showing 49 males and 31 females living in 30 dwellings.

Deane Manor, parts of which are known to date back to the 12th century stands in 70 acres of ground. It has had various owners, William of Wykeham, Bishop of Winchester in 1369 and Sir James Deane, who, under his will, established the Almshouses in Basingstoke, from the end of the 16th century. In 1864 the Manor was purchased by William Wither Bramston Beach. It remained as a home for various members of the Beach family until shortly after the death of Ellice Hicks Beach in September 1948. It was then let briefly until the Baring family acquired it in the 1950s.

During the Second World War, Royal Engineers were stationed at Home Farm, Deane with their caterpillar tractors and eight or nine men from the village served in the Home Guard. The summer of 1942 saw the arrival of American servicemen who laid a telephone cable alongside the railway line.

48

A Walk Back In Time Through Old Oakley

Having continued through the village the road again joins the B3400 at the cross-roads leading to Steventon. On the far side is the Deane Gate Inn which is thought originally to have been another Toll House. It was however known as the Deangate Public House with Sarah Thwaites as the publican on 18th April 1891 and according to the Hants Directory of 1871 had become a public house by that date.

Back along the B3400 towards Oakley and the entrance to Oakley Hall at West Lodge is seen on the right. The main building was erected in the 1790s on the site of a former two-storey house which in 1620 had been owned by George Wither (who set up the Endowed School in Church Oakley.). It remained in that family until his great-grand daughter Henrietta Maria married Edmund Bramston in 1748. Their son who took the name Wither Bramston died in 1832 without issue and so Oakley Hall passed to William Hicks Beach. The top floor was added in 1860 when other improvements were carried out. A well at Home Farm supplied the water to the Hall, the East and West Lodges and the gardeners and Home Farm Cottages.

Deane Gate Inn Circa 1904 looking from Overton Hill

49

A Walk Back In Time Through Old Oakley

Leaving the ecclesiastical parish of Deane and returning to that of Oakley, up until 1937 Church Oakley's second Post Office (the first was further along Rectory Road) and the often photographed Blewden's Grocers would have been found on the right of Rectory Road, near the turning for Station Road. It is believed that the property, now known as The Well House, was built at the end of the 17th century. The 1841 Tithe Redemption Map shows that the property, described as a house and yard, was owned by William Beach and occupied by Robert Barrett. The 1859 Whites Gazetteer of Hampshire shows that a Mr Robert Barrett was a baker, grocer and coal dealer. By 1878 Henry Blewden occupied the property and, with his wife Caroline (a Parish Councillor from 1894 until March 1907), was described as a grocer and patent medicine dealer. Kelly's Directory of 1895 shows that by that time Henry Blewden had died and that the business of baker, grocer and Post Office was carried on by Mrs Blewden. Between 1895 and 1911 the business was transferred to her son George. He continued until the business was sold to Messrs Cooper and Field on 25th March 1923.

Mr William Cooper (one of fourteen children) previously ran a shop in Crondall and his partner, Mr Matthew Field changed the name to Cooper and Field. Apart from extending into hardware and haberdashery, the main business remained that of baker, grocer and Post Office.

Post Office next to St Leonards Church

A Walk Back In Time Through Old Oakley

Although steam ovens had been installed, for some of the bread–making a faggot oven was retained for customers who preferred the old fashioned oven bottomed 'cottage loaf'. Local deliveries of bread and groceries were made with two vans and a pony cart. Harold Wheeler (who lives in Eastbourne and is Brian Wheeler's uncle) carried out some of the deliveries and Doug Harwood a resident of one of the Petersfield bungalows was one of the delivery boys.

During the early years of Cooper and Field the building remained in the ownership of the Hicks Beach family and the 1933 auction document described the property as:

'Brick built and tiles, part hanging tiles, containing five bedrooms, two attics, two sitting rooms, kitchen, large scullery, larder, shop and office. Well of water and motor pump. Company's electric lighting.

Outside are bake house and loft. Range of old brick and thatched buildings, comprising two garages, stable for two, box, coal and coke houses. Range of wood and corrugated sheds, paddock, good garden in all about 1 acre 3 rods 14 poles'.

As the lease was due to expire in 1937 Mr Field built the property now known by all the local residents as Oakley Post Office.

Running the Post Office 100 years ago appears to have taken up as many working hours as it does today although, obviously, the type of business has changed. It would appear from the Parish Council Minute Books that the proprietors of the Post Office had to seek permission to alter opening hours etc. For example it is recorded in the minutes of the meeting held on 28th March 1896 that permission was given to close the Post Office at 6 pm on Thursdays during the summer, whereas at their meeting on 14th March 1923 the Parish Council objected to the discontinuance of Saturday evening collection – 'as it would cause considerable inconvenience to the businessmen of the Parish'. On 26th March 1931 the Parish Council had no objection to the Postmaster's half–day holiday on a Saturday afternoon but it was thought that a last collection at 5.30 pm to be much too early and requested that it should be no earlier than 6.30 pm.

In addition to the Post Office the premises also contained Oakley's telephone exchange and the Blewden's were the proud possessors of the telephone number: Oakley 1. Of course the exchange was nothing like the modern one housed in the brick–built building nearly opposite the North Waltham turning. The Blewdens, and then Messrs Cooper and Field, were on call 24 hours a day, 365 days a year to connect callers. The exchange was automated just before the move to the current premises in 1937. Telegrams were also received at the Post Office for the surrounding area and an errand boy was employed to deliver them.

G. BLEWDEN, BAKER & GROCER, Post Office, OAKLEY, And at NORTH WALTHAM. Telephone, No. 1, OAKLEY. FAMILIES WAITED ON DAILY. YOUR KIND RECOMMENDATION SOLICITED

1922 advert

51

A Walk Back In Time Through Old Oakley

Making a small detour into Station Road, there are modern houses on the right. These stand on the site of five cottages which stood behind the school and were demolished early this century. Apart from these and the modern house on the left, this end of Station Road has changed very little.

In the 1891 Census James Gordon Balch, the great grandfather of a present Oakley resident, a carpenter on the Oakley Hall Estate and one of the first Parish Councillors for Church Oakley, is shown to be living in one of the five cottages sill standing on the left owned at that time by the Beach family.

On the right is what today is known as Park Farm. Back in the period when the Tithe Redemption Map of 1841 was prepared, Mr Thomas Dicker owned and occupied the farm and as appears to have been the custom it was then known as Dicker's Farm. By 1878 it was being farmed by Mr Richard Awbery and its name had changed to The Chestnuts. The 1891 Census shows that it still retained that name but a Mr Lot Lawford was in residence and he allowed youngsters to play football on one of his fields. By 1911 the farm had changed owners again to Mr J Davey. The present owners, the Small's, originally Mr Frederick Donald Small and now his son Michael took over the farm in 1929 and changed its name to Park Farm. The farmhouse is believed to have been built in the 16th century and added to in 1801.

Cottages behind Oakley School with Station Road in front, circa 1902

5 and 6 Station Road

A Walk Back In Time Through Old Oakley

Returning to Rectory Road and turning left, the next important site is Oakley Manor on the right. The ownership of the land and previous buildings has been traced back, at the instigation of its present owner, Mr Robert Priestley, to 1354. Between 1589 and 1894 it was owned by Gilbert Wither and his descendants, the Bramstons and the Hicks Beaches. Architectural evidence would indicate that The Manor was built or rebuilt prior to 1795. It is known that The Manor was extended at some time shortly before 1920 but at this time the house still had no piped water. In 1932 it was sold to an insurance company, the Cirencester Conservative Benefit Society. On 30th November 1933 The Manor was bought by Mr Robert Hunter and his wife, the Honourable Elaine Augusta Hunter for £4,410. Further alterations were carried out in 1935 with the Manor Barn being converted to Barn Cottage and Barn House. Until this time the house, then called White Walls, to the left of St Leonards Church also formed part of the estate. At one point during the 1950s the White House was lived in by Lady Warmington. During the Second World War most of the remaining estate was sold to a company and was lived in by the 16th Earl of Perth. As Sir Eric Drummond, in 1919 he was the first Secretary–General of The League of Nations. Thereafter it was owned for 17 years by Mr & Mrs Comar Wilson until its present owners bought The Manor in 1965.

Oakley Manor

What is thought to have been one of the oldest buildings in Oakley, before its demolition in the 1960s, was the Thatched Cottage standing in the grounds of the Manor. Believed to have been constructed in the 16th century it was possibly the village inn.

Old maps of the area show that the entrance to The Manor was at one time opposite Manor Cottages, one of which housed Oakley's first Post Office. In 1841 these cottages were owned by William Beach and occupied by William Goodall and James Moore. *Whites Gazetteer of Hampshire* published in 1859 shows that there was a Post Office at William Goodall's and William Wells was the Post Master in 1871. However, although the property was still described as The Post Office in the 1891 Census, William Wells' occupation is that of 'labourer on estate' and therefore it is assumed that, by that time, the business had been transferred to the Blewdens.

Yewbank also appears on the 1841 Tithe Redemption Map however, at that time it was unoccupied. Its most notable resident was Sir Harold Gillies who was presented with wrought-iron gates for the entrance to the driveway by colleagues on the staff at Park Prewitt Hospital.

On the site of the present telephone exchange in 1841 there were thatched cottages owned by John Wigg, one of which was occupied by Ann Appleton. Next to these the Parish Room or Reading Room was later built. It was of a similar construction as East Oakley Village Hall and was for many years used for a variety of village activities such as the Womens Institute, Mothers Union, Guides and Scouts and during the Second World War was used as an evacuee assembly and dispersal point. During the time that Rev Hume was Rector the playing of cards in the hall was banned and he also objected to the singing of harmless comic songs at concerts. Following the building of the Andover Road Village Hall the Reading Room became less popular and it was dismantled and taken to Kempshott where it became their village hall for several years.

On the opposite corner of the track leading to the Peter Houseman playing field is Sunbeam Cottage. The original building on this site dates back to before the time of George Wither who was alive in the 17th century. The present cottage was rebuilt by Mr Wither Bramston in 1825 with two free-standing octagonal rooms constructed in the garden, one of which (now demolished) was a stable where the horses stood with their heads facing the centre of the room. It was used for many years as a cramming establishment (see the chapter on schools).

Opposite Sunbeam Cottage is a lane leading to the A30 near to Dummer. The name of this lane has caused a certain amount of controversy over the years. Names which have come to light during our research for this book include Dummer Lane, Trenchards Lane, Beech Lane and Waltham Road.

BEECH LANE OAKLEY

Set back from the lane, opposite the turning for North Waltham, is Bulls Bushes Farm. The farmhouse is believed to be late Georgian or early Victorian (1839 is engraved on the garden wall). There are two large cellars under the main part of the house – one containing a huge wooden table which was actually built in the cellar and is too large to be removed. The cellars were used as a dairy for making cheese and setting cream etc and have heavy wooden shelves around the side. Mrs Passmore, the present owner, has been told that under the present kitchen floor (constructed in about 1900) there are two huge brick water tanks with domed tops which were used to drain water from the house roof. There was a pump in the kitchen to take the water to the storage tank in the attic. Further domed brick water tanks have been found – one under a building at the end of the milking sheds which had slate shelves and signs of a fire of some kind in the corner, another which has been preserved was found when building a new barn and a final one in the back yard of the cottages.

Beech Lane with Reading Room and thatched cottages on the right, and one of three village street lamps on the other side of the road. Circa 1915

Aerial view of Bull Bushes Farm showing Old Barn with wooden shingle tiled roof on the left in front of barn with domed roof.

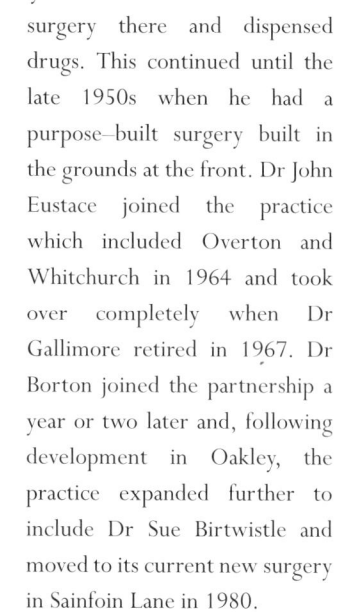

The cottages were originally four dwellings, one having just the downstairs rooms for a single man who ate with the family next door. They were converted firstly into three cottages and then at sometime between 1964 and 1968, into two. When the family arrived in 1968 there was a huge old barn with a wooden shingle tiled roof which had originally been thatched, a brick–built stable block, coach houses, and tack room which was used as the headquarters of one of the Home Guard Units during the Second World War.

The farm appears on the 1841 Tithe Redemption Map as being owned by William Beach and occupied by John Taplin. Thomas Crighton was the tenant in 1859, Alfred Rumboll in 1878 and Frances Grear at the time of the 1891 Census. From the various directories consulted it appears that the farm changed hands several times before the present owners, the Passmore family from Sussex, purchased the farm in 1968.

Returning to Rectory Road there are some houses on the right, the second of which was built for Dr Gallimore in the 1930s. He not only lived in the house but had his surgery there and dispensed drugs. This continued until the late 1950s when he had a purpose–built surgery built in the grounds at the front. Dr John Eustace joined the practice which included Overton and Whitchurch in 1964 and took over completely when Dr Gallimore retired in 1967. Dr Borton joined the partnership a year or two later and, following development in Oakley, the practice expanded further to include Dr Sue Birtwistle and moved to its current new surgery in Sainfoin Lane in 1980.

A little further along on the left is the present Oakley Post Office still trading under the name of Cooper and Field the original owners. Mr Field had the new premises built in 1937 on land originally owned by Garretts the undertakers when Mr Cooper retired. Unfortunately both Mr & Mrs Field had died by the early part of the Second World War and Mr Cooper came out of retirement until his son Norman, returned from serving six and half years in the Army in 1946.

For several years many of the commodities such as sugar, dried fruit etc came in sacks so that everything had to be weighed and re–wrapped before being sold in the shop or delivered to customers. Before the expansion of the village all the mail was delivered from Basingstoke and sorted by two postmen and Mr Cooper before it was delivered in the village. At Christmas time sorting started at 4 am so that all the additional mail could be dealt with.

A Walk Back In Time Through Old Oakley

When Mr and Mrs Cooper retired on 1st September 1981 Brian (whose mother was the daughter of the original Mr Cooper) and Margaret Wheeler purchased the business and, whilst modernising the interior and specialising in many locally produced items, they have retained the personal service which many of the older customers had been used to and have gained the reputation of being the 'Fortnum and Mason's of Oakley'. In latter years Mrs Wheeler has diversified her business interests and now also runs a reputable guest house.

Opposite Cooper and Field are the Old Malthouses which appear on the map of the village of 1845 when one was owned by William Budd and the other by Anne Allen. Nothing much more is known about these cottages except that they were used as dormitories for the young gentlemen attending the cramming establishment at what is now Sunbeam Cottage.

Post Office in Rectory Road. Photograph was taken before the addition of the front extension and when the Post Box was on the left of the door

A Walk Back In Time Through Old Oakley

On the same side of the road is East Oakley House which appears to date back to pre–1761 when the property was in the hands of William Budd. The map of 1845 shows that John Taplin was the owner and occupier of the property described in his Will dated 28th November 1849, as Home Farm. John Taplin died on 3rd March 1851 and, although his wife Sarah continued to live at the house until her death on 7th April 1863, the Whites Gazetteer of Hampshire, published in 1859, shows Thomas Hide as the farmer. In September 1863 the property was sold to James White a cattle dealer of Broad Oak, Odiham. The 1891 Census and the 1895 *Kellys Directory* show Ernest Lamb as residing at the farm. Early this century the property was known as Folletts Farm and was occupied by Samuel Crowder. It was subsequently converted into a private residence by Dr Duckenfield Scott MA LLD FRS, a keen botanist who was responsible for planting the gardens with many exotic plants. Although the exact dates of ownership are unknown, the various directories between 1915 and 1939 show Dr Scott as being at East Oakley House.

During the Second World War former residents of Hill Road can remember often seeing members of the Ulster Searchlight Battalion, who were stationed at Breach Farm, walking through the village with their towels over their arms, making their way to East Oakley House to have a bath at the invitation of Lady Crawley.

East Oakley House, a view from the rear garden laid out by Dr Scott – a noted botanist

A Walk Back In Time Through Old Oakley

From 1949 until the latter part of 1993, the property was owned by the Onslow–Fane family who continued the practise of allowing many village events to be held in the thatched barn situated at the front of the house. A custom which appears to have been started by Dr Scott.

We have now arrived back at where our walk started – at East Oakley pond, but we still have a little further to go before we have explored the whole of old Oakley.

The cottages surrounding the pond have changed little in appearance over the years except for Alan's Folly and Forge Cottage. The latter, it is believed, housed a bake–house where villagers took their meals to be cooked at 1d per meal. This may have been part of Mrs Phillips shop listed in *Kellys Directory* of 1895. Even the newer residents of the village will remember the collapse of the end of the Forge one summer's night a few years ago. Although the demise of the building was a loss, it provided the strip of land for the much–needed footway between Oakley Lane and Oakley Post Office in Rectory Road to be constructed.

T Garrett, Shoeing Smith, Builder, Wheelwright and Undertaker – at The Forge in Oakley Lane in the early 1900s

A Walk Back In Time Through Old Oakley

Although one could be forgiven for thinking that the Forge was always the site of the village blacksmith, records show that the blacksmiths shop was in the yard behind The Lilacs (now 5 Oakley Lane where Mr Kent the dentist lives). It later moved to the Forge and was at different times owned by William Phillips (1895 *Kellys Directory*), T Garrett (1915 *Kellys Directory*) and Alfred Smith (1931 and 1939 editions). It finally closed in 1950.

The site behind 'The Lilacs' has also been the premises for various businesses over the years. One of the most well known being Huntleys Buses which was started in the 1930s. It was also used by T & J Garrett as their workshop. They were carpenters and wheelwrights and, at one stage, they were also the village undertakers. Later the same premises were used by Mr Frank Garrett who was an upholsterer.

On the far side of the pond to the left of the Primitive Methodist Chapel is Alan's Folly. This was originally two cottages said to be owned by Elizabeth Blackburn at the time of the 1841 Tithe Redemption Award Map and later by Richard Blackburn who sold the plot of land (then known as Railway Croft) on which the Primitive Methodist Chapel was built. The cottages with 14–inch thick walls, constructed of a chalk mix, became so decayed that they were condemned. After the Second World War Mr Herbert Lewis undertook the conversion of the 'Folly' and it was renamed after his grandson Alan. The present timber–frame appearance dates back to the conversion.

The cottages at The Pond taken after the snowstorm on 25th April 1908. From left: The Lilacs, Pond Cottage, Olcote and Alan's Folly

A Walk Back In Time Through Old Oakley

Barley Mow circa 1960, with Oakley Stores to the left of the trees, behind which lies Deepwell Cottage

Standing in the corner is Olcote which was built prior to 1841 and is believed to have been a grocers shop owned by Mr Thomas Porter at the time of the 1891 Census and the publication of the 1895 *Kellys Directory*. It later became the home of Miss Violet Peters, the daughter of one of the Headmasters of Oakley School. In the early 1950s it was occupied by Mr F Garrett, a carpenter. The somewhat strange name is said to have derived from the initial letters of 'Our little corner of this earth'.

To the left is Pond Cottage which, prior to conversion, was two cottages with a lower roof. It was the home for a while of Tom Garrett of T & J Garrett.

Leaving the pond area you pass Elm Cottage on the left and Ivy Cottage, the birthplace of Jack Garrett's father in 1879 and his grandfather before that, on the right. The terrace of cottages on the left leading to the Barley Mow are also mentioned in the 1841 Tithe Redemption Award. One of them appears to have been owned by John Taplin (who also owned what is now East Oakley House) and occupied by William Tickle. 'Ref' Garrett lived in the first of the chalk cottages.

The Barley Mow also dates back to pre–1841 when it was owned by John Kidgell and occupied by Mary Lovegrove, also it is believed that, at one time the beer for the inn was brewed in the cottage opposite.

A Walk Back In Time Through Old Oakley

Deepwell Cottage as it appears in 1994

By 1859 it would appear that William Hunt was the landlord and the 1891 Census shows that he was still the publican some 32 years later. By 1903 the business was, according to *Kellys Directory*, under the name of Miss Harriet Hunt. The Neale family moved to the Barley Mow in 1918. At that time there was one bar called the Smoking Room. The Tap Room with a larger bar was opened later. The land was also used by an annual Travelling Fair with coconut shies, roundabouts and swingboats. It is said that a chicken farm was at one time situated in what is now the Junior School Playing Field.

Opposite is the Grade II listed building – Deepwell Cottage, reputed to be the oldest cottage in the village. Research by John Bonner, the present owner, shows that it was probably built about 1450. It was built of Cruck construction and very few dwellings of that type remain today. The cottage still has two wattle and daub internal wall sections in the roof, the open roof trusses that would have been the centre of the hall remain and one set of Cruck oak beams still show evidence of being scorched by the fire burning on the hearth as the smoke escaped through a louvre in the roof. Deepwell Cottage appears on a map of Oakley dated circa 1600. In 1845 the cottage was owned by the Rev Lovelace Bigg–Wither and occupied by James Harmsworth. However, because most of the dwellings on the 1891 Census were described as 'cottage' and no road names were indicated, it is not possible to trace its owner 100 years ago.

A Walk Back In Time Through Old Oakley

To the left of Deepwell Cottage, close to the entrance to The Vale, there was another pond. This served as an overflow for the one outside the Methodist Chapel, and in bad weather, it was not unusual to see water running down the then much narrower Oakley Lane between the two.

There has been a shop on the site of 'One–Stop' for many years. Mr Thompson preceded Mr Saunders, who many people living in the village in the 1940s will remember, as the shopkeeper. During Mr Saunders' time deliveries were made to customers on a regular basis. Then the shop entrance faced Oakley Lane which was far narrower and more dusty than now, with nut trees nearly meeting overhead. In the early 1950s a butcher's section was opened at the rear of the building (where the frozen food cabinets can now be found) and in July 1966 it was changed to the mini super–market that it is today. The other shops were then built and the well, situated below what is now the hairdressers, was filled in.

Before Oakley Lane was widened in the 1970s it took the line of what is now the school layby. At the far end of the layby, behind a high laurel hedge, is South View.

South View, Oakley Lane, circa 1910, showing Jack, Betty, Bernard, Donald and Harold Wheeler in the garden

63

A Walk Back In Time Through Old Oakley

As mentioned in the chapter on schools, late last century South View was a junior boarding school. In the early 1900s it was bought by Mr W Wheeler. His son Don (Brian's father) was born there and the family remained at South View until 1956 when the daughter Betty and her husband Henry Tarrant sold it.

On the other side of the lane is 32 Oakley Lane, the site of Doltons Garage and Jeans the Florist.

Doltons Garage was started by Ernest Dolton in the 1930s. He had married Elizabeth Saunders who had been in service at Malshanger and had earlier started a fish delivery round. The business in Oakley Lane started with Ernest Dolton making paraffin deliveries from a 40-gallon drum with a horse and cart. He expanded into charging radio batteries with a charging shed at the rear of the property. Next came his Raleigh Bicycle agency, the sale of petrol from a single petrol pump and car repairs.

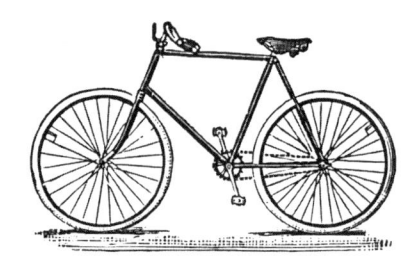

Doltons Garage in the 1950s, showing old petrol pumps and 'open for business'

A Walk Back In Time Through Old Oakley

Mr & Mrs Dolton remained at No 32 for twenty years until he transferred the business to his daughter, Violet and son–in law, Arthur Hunt The business further diversified into a taxi and wedding car hire business and later a hardware business was started in part of the house now occupied by Jeans the Florist.

In about 1964 Vi Hunt and her daughter Jean McCombie started a wool and haberdashery shop in the newly constructed single–storey building which now houses the DIY and hardware businesses. When Vi and Arthur Hunt retired the whole property was split between their two children Alan Hunt and Jean McCombie. Jean became the owner of the house and transferred her wool and haberdashery business into that building. She added the sale of ladies and children's clothes and floristry later. As the floristry business grew it needed more space and it moved into the area it now currently occupies. The flower business was transferred to the current owner in 1987 and Applebys the Estate Agents opened in 1988.

The petrol, DIY and hardware side of the Doltons Garage business is continued by Keith Baker and Hugh Temple.

The route then continues down Oakley Lane towards the railway bridge. Years ago the scenery would have looked very different. On the right, just past the turning for Kennett Way, were Marlborough Villas.

Oakley Lane circa 1960, before it was widened, looking towards the railway bridge with Marlborough Villas on the right

A Walk Back In Time Through Old Oakley

Nearly opposite was the yard used by T and J Garrett who were builders and undertakers. They later moved to premises behind 'The Lilacs'.

On the land in the area now known as Highland Drive was a large house known as Highlands. It was for a time owned by Mr Fookes a poultry farmer, and the last owner prior to it being sold for development in the early 1970s, was Mr Seeney previously the owner of the Beach Arms Garage.

Also built along Oakley Lane were nine out of a total of thirty five tin bungalows. These were built circa 1910 (certainly before the First World War) by a company known as Homesteads. One of those tin bungalows called Ashley was in 1924 occupied by the family of five year–old Fred Brickell whose uncle Tom Dibben was the owner of Upper Farm and Mrs Norman Coopers grandfather. The bungalow stood on the right immediately before the railway bridge.

T & J Garrett's yard, Oakley Lane

Most of the bungalows were constructed to the same design. Inside the back door was a room, approximately eight by six feet, with an earth floor which was used to store fire wood, paraffin and coal (then it was 1/11d a cwt ie less than 10p). The expensive ones had a copper for boiling the clothes. The next room was the living room with a black kitchen range which was blackened with lead, the mouldings were polished with emery cloth and the hearth was whitened with a lump of chalk and water, this was done every day. The front door opened into the living room, and so did all three bedroom doors.

Every–day life was very much different in those days. Paraffin lamps or candles were used for lighting. The lamps had glass hoods which would crack if the wick was turned up too quickly. As glass hoods cost 6d, a hair pin would be hung over the top which was supposed to help prevent the glass from cracking. Children had to go bed early to save the candles. The people who could afford them, had what was called Aladdin Lamps which used a mantle similar to the gas mantle.

For cooking, the kitchen range which had an oven for baking the bread and cakes was used. If this had not been lit in the morning, water was boiled by means of a Primus stove. On a Monday, which was always washday, the man of the house would fill and light the copper before he left for work.

The sanitary arrangements were an outside loo with a bucket which had to be emptied every week by digging a hole in the garden (making sure that it was not dug in the same place as the week before). It was usually the job of the youngest member of the family to make sure there was a supply of newspaper hung on the inside of the door. This had to be cut into squares, a hole pierced in the corner and threaded on a piece of string.

At that time there was no mains water or electricity anywhere in the area. There were eleven wells in the village, which certain properties were allowed to use. The remainder of the properties had either water barrels or underground tanks which stored all the rain water collected from the roof. This had to be boiled before drinking but it made a delicious cup of tea.

The rest of the thirty–five bungalows were built in St Johns Road (3), Pardown (8), Barn Lane (2), Pack Lane (7), Andover Road (5) and Grub Lane (3). Most of these survived until the expansion of Oakley in the 1960s but only one now remains in Oakley Lane, to the left of the Police House.

It is interesting to note that East Oakley Village Hall was built in the same period and of the same construction which shows just how sturdy these buildings were. Back in 1930 it was possible to purchase one of the tin bungalows and ten acres of land for about £1,000.

The tin bungalow has now been replaced by the Brickell company's offices. On 5th December 1945, Brickell's bought the wheelwright, carpenters and under–taking business carried on by Thomas Garrett. Whilst continuing with the original business they expanded into building bungalows and renovation work. In 1959, in conjunction with Hampshire County Council, they started building swimming pools for schools (including the one at Oakley Junior School). The undertakers part of the business was sold to Spencer and Peyton Limited in 1960. The company now has branches in Gloucestershire and Guernsey. One of the most prestigious pieces of work they have undertaken was the building of a swimming pool for the Prince of Wales at Highgrove, for this job they were awarded the Royal Warrant.

Under the railway and set back to the left of Oakley Lane with their vehicular entrance in Lightsfield was the business known as 'The Farmers' Friend', the trading name of Perry's of Oakley Limited. Mr Tom Perry started the business operating from a small workshop with a car and trailer offering a mobile repair service for farm machinery. He then began to develop jog troughs and elevators to his own design. The company soon became known all over the world for their machinery with its distinctive yellow colour and particularly for their efforts in helping local farmers in all respects from repairs, to grain and materials handling, complete grain storage layouts etc. Most of the equipment was made at their factory in Oakley. The company closed its doors in Oakley for the last time several years ago and relocated to Devon.

Although the walk ends here, the life of the village continues. The next 100 years will no doubt see further changes to the village again, but one thing we hope never alters is the community spirit and friendliness of its inhabitants.

High Days And Holidays: Notable Events

As with any village, national events during the last one hundred years have been celebrated in various forms locally. These include coronations, jubilees and, of course, the end of the two World Wars.

The Silver Jubilee of King George V, celebrated in 1935, included a procession of villagers led by a donkey. This was followed by a parade of decorated prams and bicycles and a 'large baby in a large pram'. Entertainment took the form of sports, a Punch and Judy show and a Fancy Dress Dance. The celebrations ended with a Bonfire, and refreshments included a sit down tea in a large marquee.

The Coronation of King George VI and Queen Elizabeth on 12th May 1937 was marked by a special service in St Leonards Church in the morning. An afternoon and evening of fun followed. Villagers enjoyed various sports, a comic football match, ladies versus gentlemen tug–'o'–war in the Glebe Field, rounded off with tea and dancing. The day ended with a bonfire and fireworks display. It would appear that most residents attended these activities.

Fancy Dress Football in the Glebe Field to celebrate the Coronation of King George VI and Queen Elizabeth in 1937. Standing from left: Harold Seeney, (?), Ernie Dolton, Bill Collis, (?), (?), Monty Hunt Bottom row from left: Stan Sims, Dick Warwick, Charlie Hunt, (?), (?)

High Days And Holidays: Notable Events

One of the Carnival Princesses for the Coronation Celebrations in 1953, Miss Margaret Hewlett (better known now as Mrs Wheeler at Oakley Post Office)

High Days And Holidays: Notable Events

Street party for Queen Elizabeth II Silver Jubilee in June 1977 showing some of the children sheltering from the rain under the tables

A week later there was an outing to London for the choir, bellringers, Mother's Union and other residents to see the Coronation Decorations (Canon Jeudwine noted that the outing started at 3.30 pm and arrived home at about midnight).

The coronation of our present monarch Queen Elizabeth II on 2nd June 1953 was again commemorated by the holding of a service at St Leonards Church in the morning but the celebrations in the afternoon took place at the Recreation Ground at Newfound. They took the form of a Country Fair, with country and may–pole dancing and stalls and side shows, such as skittles.

The Carnival Queen who was employed at the Well House, and the two Carnival Princesses, Miss Margaret Hewlett (now better known as Mrs Wheeler at Oakley Post Office) and Miss Janet Watley, had been chosen from a number of contestants by Canon and Mrs Jeudwine, and Mr and Mrs Onslow–Fane at a gathering in their barn.

A street party organised by the Oakley Young Folks Committee, and funded by residents and local organisations, was held on 7th June 1977 to celebrate the Queen's Silver Jubilee.

It received considerable press coverage beforehand due to the problems encountered in connection with the closing of a short stretch of Oakley Lane, outside the school. In the end, although official permission was withheld, the road was closed. Despite the rain, 1,000 school–age children from Oakley, Deane, Malshanger and Newfound enjoyed the tea party and entertainment provided. The weather cleared in the evening for the tug–o'–war, disco and barbecue. In addition to the party, each local school child received a commemorative mug from the Parish Council.

High Days And Holidays: Notable Events

Group of boys circa 1915 Another similar photograph is that taken of ladies and children at Oakley Hall about 1926.

The next time street parties were seen in Oakley was for the wedding of the Prince of Wales and Lady Diana Spencer in July 1981. Although not on the grand scale of the one in 1977, most areas held their own festivities. In addition people stood on the railway bridges at either end of 'The Drive' to wave to the Royal Train as it carried the couple to Romsey for the start of their honeymoon.

People from the village also took part in events outside the area. One such event was the Diocesan Missionary Pageant held at Old Basing in 1931, when 56 Oakley residents took part.

It is obvious from postcards and photographs that many other events took place in the early part of this century on which very little information is available. One such postcard is of a group of boys which was produced in circa 1915. Although there is no further information, the correspondence on the reverse provides an insight into the pace of life at that time. The card was sent to Mrs H Biddlecombe who lived in Langton Road, Boscombe by her sister, Mrs Chant of Court Cottage in Oakley Lane and read:

> 'My Dear S, I have today sent you by rail a few Black Berrys, carriage paid to Boscombe Station so if you do not receive them very early you might just fetch them. you may please yourself if you care to give Jim any of them. There are a few plums in the bottom of basket – I hope they wont be crushed, Jim and Clifford picked them today where these are is Jim and Clifford in photo. C looks frightened. Baby walks nicely now'.

High Days And Holidays: Notable Events

Ladies and children at Oakley Hall circa 1926. The picture includes: Mrs Brown with her young sons, Ron and Bruce (bottom left), Dolly, Gladys and Eva Neale (centre) Mrs Garrett with grandson Dennis on lap

Diocesan Missionary Pageant held at Old Basing circa 1931
Top row from left: (?), (?), Mrs Jeudwine, (?), Mr Fitch,
Bottom row from left: Roy Butler, Mrs Chard, Violet Fowle, Frank Wyatt, (?), Mena Lee

High Days And Holidays: Notable Events

Garrett family wedding circa 1902
Top row: Second from left: Alf Garrett, wheelwright and carpenter, next to him 'Ref' Garrett who lived at 11 Oakley Lane Second row: Third from left: Tom Garrett, wheelwright, carpenter, and undertaker who lived at Pond Cottage, Sitting: Middle child: Thomas Garrett, Tom Garrett's son fourth from left: William Garrett, undertaker and wheelwright

Weddings were often a great event to which many members of the bride and groom's families came, along with many villagers.

Although the formal wedding photograph has not changed over the years, the style of recording the event in the local newspaper has. Whereas today only the very briefest of details are reported in the local paper, back in the 1920s every minute detail of the day was recorded for all to read. We have been fortunate to have been lent a scrapbook of newspaper cuttings in respect of events occurring in Oakley and reported in the *Hants & Berks. Gazette.*

Below is the report of the wedding of Mr Harold Wheeler and Miss Gweneth Winnett as it appeared in that paper on Friday 14th June 1929.

'**WEDDING** – The wedding took place on Saturday, at the Parish Church, of Mr. Harold Charles Wheeler, third son of Mr and Mrs W Wheeler, of East Oakley, and Miss Gweneth Winnett, only daughter of Mr and Mrs W H Winnett, of Pardown, East Oakley. Both families reside in the village, and much interest was taken in the ceremony, a large congregation being present at the church, where the bride has for many years been a member of the choir. The bride, who was given away by her father, wore a white satin dress with diamante trimmings, and a wreath of orange blossom with veil. She carried a shower bouquet of pink carnations. Her pearl necklet was the gift of the bridegroom. She was attended by two bridesmaids, Misses Molly and Peggy Wyeth (cousins of the bridegroom), who wore blue marocain dresses and beige crinoline hats trimmed with blue georgette. They carried bouquets of blue iris and love–in–the–mist, and wore gold brooches, the gifts of the bridegroom. The duties of best man were carried out by Mr. John Wheeler. The Rector (Rev G H Jeudwine) officiated, and the organist was Mr. Charles Paragreen, Mus. Bac. (from London). The service was choral, the hymns sung being 'Love divine, all loves excelling,' and 'The voice that breathed o'er Eden.' Mr. Paragreen played the organ Fantasia in C by Berthold Tours and Mendelssohn's Wedding March. After the ceremony the reception was held at The Woodlands, Pardown, among those present in addition to the parents of the bride and bridegroom being Mr and Mrs J Wyeth, Mrs A W Wyeth, Miss Wheeler, Messrs B and D Wheeler, Mrs Morgan, Mr and Mrs Paragreen, Mr and Mrs Trewinard (Richmond), Mr and Mrs Phillimore, Mrs Russell, and Misses M and B Lee. The happy couple left at 4.15 pm for Brighton for the honeymoon, the bride's travelling dress being pink silk with tweed coat and beige crinoline hat'.

The report continues with a complete list of the gifts and who gave them.

High Days And Holidays: Notable Events

Before the present era, where practically every household owns a car, events to which many people looked forward to going on, were the Huntley Bus outings. Every Sunday, during the summer, a coach load of men, women and children left the village for a trip to the seaside, either to Hayling Island or Southsea and at other times during the year outings for The Fox Inn Darts Team, and the cricket and football teams were arranged. One of the favourite drivers for these occasions was Doug Harwood who drove for Mr Huntley for many years and still lives in the village.

The Church Fête both in Deane and Oakley has been a well-attended attraction in both villages for many years.

Following the arrival of Hilsea College, Deane's Church Fête was for many years held in their grounds at Oakley Hall.

Oakley School Country Dancers – circa 1928 (Perhaps these girls performed at the early Oakley fêtes)
Standing from left: Cassie Beaver, Evelyn Hunt, Lilly Neville, Doris Chant, Kathy Wootton, Vi Hunt, Ethel Stockwell, Queenie Eckett, Olive Harwood, Hilda Garrett, Winnie Fowle
Seated from left: Winnie Mullins, Edith Owen, Grace Irwin (teacher), Ida Baker, Nellie Heans

High Days And Holidays: Notable Events

Huntley's Bus outing circa 1950, believed to be The Fox Inn Darts Team Outing
Back row from left: Doug Harwood (coach driver), Mrs Harwood, Pop Spicer (Landlord of the Fox Inn), Mr George Faulkner (coach driver), Harold Nutley, Margaret Goodall, Charlie Mears, Horace Kearsley with twins Malcolm and Christine standing in front
Front row from left: Arthur Annetts, Frank Goodall on shoulders of Bert Lawrence, (?)

High Days And Holidays: Notable Events

The first record we have of Oakley's fête is 1921 when it was held at Summerdown Meadow. The Band of the Kings Own Rifles played. The next one was at the same venue on 14th July 1923 and raised £80. This was shared equally between the School Extension Fund and Basingstoke Cottage Hospital.

Since then the fêtes have been held at a variety of sites over the years, including Oakley Hall in the 1920s and 30s, Malshanger in the late 1930s, Oakley Manor (late 1930s), The Rectory (during the war years) and East Oakley House. In more recent times it has been held in Church Meadow, Peter Houseman Field and this year, for the first time, at St Johns Youth Centre.

1976 saw the Fête opened by Oakley's first Carnival Queen, Miss Jane Milton from the Beach Arms Hotel.

Another similar event which now has a permanent place in the village calendar is the May Fayre, held on the first Monday in May at the Peter Houseman Field. This is organised by the Premises Committee of the Oakley Scouts and Guides to raise funds for the maintenance of their headquarters at St Johns Piece.

The village also joined in other national and local events which were not such joyous occasions but still a part of the social history of our village.

Several such events during World War II recorded in Canon Jeudwine's notebook entitled 'some Parish Records' show that Oakley has always had an extremely generous nature.

During the week of 17th to 24th May 1941, designated War Weapons Week, Oakley's contribution was just over £3,000 (a tremendous sum in 1994, let alone in 1941).

In 1943 the people of Oakley raised £103.15.0d (£103.75) for the Red Cross Fund for Prisoners of War. The Wings for Victory Appeal held later that year received £2,054 from the village of which £321.2.0d was raised by the school.

In this the 50th anniversary year of D–Day the report of 'salute the Soldier Week' held between 3rd and 10th June 1944 is of particular interest. Various sports meetings, whist drives, a concert and a social and dance were held during that period, concluding with a Church Parade for the Home Guard and Civil Defence at the morning service on Sunday 11th. Once again a splendid sum of £2,688 was raised.

In 1940, a platoon which became part of 'B' Company of the 3rd (Hampshire Battalion of the Home Guard was formed of volunteers from Oakley, Malshanger and the surrounding neighbourhood under the command of Mr Sturges.

Watcher's posts were soon established and nightly patrols protected Battledown Flyover. Later, the Platoon was divided into Malshanger Platoon (with Wootton and Deane) and Oakley Platoon. The Home Guard had their headquarters at Oakley Village Hall. Sunday mornings and Wednesday evenings were given up to drills, exercises and lectures and many 'mock battles' were fought in the woods around the village.

High Days And Holidays: Notable Events

George Smith (left) and A Goodyear (right) in their Home Guard uniforms

Camp Fires And Camaraderie:
Oakley's Youth Organisations

An important part of village life has always been those organisations through the membership of which the young people can channel their seemingly infinite energy and enthusiasm.

Following that first Scout Camp held on Brownsea Island back in 1908, the framework was set to provide every community in the United Kingdom with such organisations – the Scout and Guide Movements. It appears that Oakley was no exception in taking up the challenge and below is a resumé of the formation of what remains today a very active section of the village.

Brownies: There had been a Brownie Pack in the village before 1914, but unfortunately there is no information about it. The next reference to this organisation is in Canon Jeudwine's notebook where it is recorded that Mrs Ridges (the wife of the Headmaster of Oakley School) was enrolled as Brown Owl on 27th July 1922. The number of young girls enrolled as Brownies gradually increased and it is believed that it was only disbanded, like many other organisations, on the outbreak of the Second World War.

The Pack was reformed in 1957/8 by Mrs Frankham (who still lives in the village) and met at East Oakley Village Hall. Since then they met at a variety of locations, (St Leonards Centre, St Johns Church, and the Onslow Fane Hall), until 1982 when before the new Scout and Guide Headquarters was built at St Johns Piece.

On Mrs Frankham's retirement Mrs Joan Baulch took over as a Brownie Guider of a very large Pack and with the growth of the village it was decided to open a second Pack. Further expansion of the village saw the number of Brownie Packs increase to five and at the time of writing a total of four Packs continue to exist.

Girl Guides: The first record of a Girl Guide Company in Oakley is in 1922 when Miss Chute the District Commissioner gave her consent for Mrs Jeudwine to undertake the Captain's work. On 28th July of that year eleven girls were enrolled and the Robin, Swallow and Canary Patrols were formed. Their meeting place was the barn in front of East Oakley House and their equipment was transported between there and The Rectory on a handcart. On 20th December 1928 the Company was presented with their Company Colours, a gift from Mrs Fletcher, the District Commissioner for Brookwood.

The Second World War saw this company being disbanded but Guiding in Oakley did not cease completely. Mrs Platt of Hilsea College, continued the Girl Guide Company, started in Portsmouth, when the school and its pupils moved to the area in 1940.

Camp Fires And Camaraderie: Oakley's Youth Organisations

Oakley Brownies in 1957/58. Top row from left: Sheila Smith (Tawny Owl), Mrs Platt (District Commissioner), Mrs Frankham (Brown Owl), June Sherburn Second row from left: Wendy Stratton, Pat Franklin, Maureen Stacey, Carol Chivers, Linda Huntley, Sandra Norris, Jennifer Eastwood, Jacqueline Kent Bottom row from left: Andrea Beavis, Pamela Mundy, Katherine Fisher, Jean Frankham, Anna (?), Jill Garrett, Charmaine Choules

Oakley Girl Guides at camp in the 1920s Top row from left: (?), Winnie Fowle, Miss Jeudwine, Ida Barker, Violet Fowle Middle row from left: (?), Guide Lieutenant, Mrs Jeudwine (Captain), Helen Jeudwine Bottom row from left: (?), (?), Edith Owen

Camp Fires And Camaraderie: Oakley's Youth Organisations

In 1960 Mrs Smith restarted a Guide Company away from Hilsea College. On her departure for Australia in 1963 Mrs Ellen Cox and Mrs Joan Baulch (both still living in Pardown) became Captain and Lieutenant respectively. Their first meeting, at what is now St Leonards Centre, was held on 4th June 1964 and attended by nine Guides. Such was the popularity of the group that the number had doubled by the end of the year.

With the increase in numbers, money was needed to buy equipment and therefore a number of fund-raising events were held. The most famous was the annual Pantomime which was performed for ten consecutive years from the late 1960s. Each child in all the Guide Companies had a part in the Pantomime which ran for three evenings plus a matinee on a Saturday afternoon to which the older residents of the village and the children from Lymington House School (a school for disabled children in Basingstoke) were invited. The show was under the management of Leslie Sibthorpe and his wife Florrie who wrote many of the scripts.

Oakley Girl Guide Pantomime in 1978 Standing in front from left: Thelma Tarling, Ellen Cox, Joan Baulch, Florrie Sibthorpe, Les Sibthorpe

Rangers: A Rangers Unit for girls over fifteen years of age was formed in 1930 but again this was disbanded during the Second World War and does not appear to have been reformed.

Beavers: The first Beaver Colony in Oakley was formed in September 1983 under the leadership of 'Rusty' (*ie* Mrs Margaret Blight). Currently there are two Colonies catering for youngsters between the ages of six and eight.

Cubs: In February 1963, Mrs West started the first Cub Pack under the sponsorship of the Rev K Jackson and with the help of a Cub's mother, Mrs Brown. Meetings were held at the Oakley Infant School, which at that time was still housed in what is now St Leonards Centre and later meetings were transferred to St Johns Church before the erection of the Onslow Fane Hall. A further two Packs had been opened by the end of the 1970s and the three packs continue to flourish.

When the Basingstoke Scout District was split into 'East' and 'West' in 1979/80 the competition to design the new Basingstoke West District badge was won by an Oakley Cub Scout. Roy Shepherd, who still lives in the village, became the new District Commissioner.

In the mid 1970s the Cubs started to go carol singing around the village raising money for charity. In later years they have joined their friends in the Basingstoke West District in a Christingle Service.

Scouts: As far as we can ascertain the first Scout Troop of thirteen Scouts was formed back in 1914 with a Scout Master by the name of Mr Peters. This only ran for a short while.

The next reference to a Scout Troop in Oakley is the one run by Mr Matthew Field after his arrival at the Post Office next to the Church. It appears that meetings at this time were held at the Parish Room but no further records are available.

During the Second World War, the 54th Portsmouth Scout Troop arrived with the school at Hilsea College. Unfortunately owing to the lack of leaders, it was suspended in 1946.

In May 1968 Mr Parker from Basingstoke restarted a Scout Troop in Oakley and by the end of 1978 there were three Troops – St Johns, St Leonard and St Lawrence. Later due to lack of leaders, the St Johns and St Lawrence Troops amalgamated.

As part of their service to the Community, the Scouts started their 'Christmas Post' in the early 1980s. Christmas cards are delivered within the village at a reduced rate and free for senior citizens and the disabled. In addition, 1985 saw the first of the annual Scout Fun Runs, the brain child of the Scout Leader of St Leonards Troop, Mr D Lawrence. Individuals and teams of all ages run from the Peter Houseman Field to the Scout and Guide Headquarters to raise funds for various charities.

Oakley Boy Scouts marching outside St Leonards Church soon after the formation of the movement

Ventures: The Venture Scout Unit has been in existence since the late 1970s and has produced a considerable number of youngsters who have gained their Queen Scout Award – the highest training award in youth section of the movement.

Many of the Unit members are actively involved in the running of the other sections of the Oakley Scout Group. An additional important area of service is their aid work in less developed areas of the world. Over the years several members of the Oakley Unit have volunteered to help in such areas as Kenya, Russia and Sri Lanka.

Scout and Guide Headquarters: In the early days of Scouting and Guiding in the village the meetings were held in a variety of locations and it was not until 1972/73 that they had their own hall. This was known as the Onslow Fane Hall and was erected on land owned by Mr Jack Onslow Fane and Mr Robert Priestley on the right at the top of the 'old' part of Barn Lane. The building was by no means new having previously been a Roman Catholic Church and later a naval barracks at Gosport. After raising about £1,000 by staging various events the hut was bought from *HMS Collingwood* for £100, dismantled and rebuilt on its new site. Volunteers refurbished the building so that it contained a large main hall, a kitchen, toilets, an office, and two storage rooms.

Camp Fires And Camaraderie: Oakley's Youth Organisations

Jack Onslow Fane at the opening of the Onslow Fane Hall in Barn Lane either side of him are Ellen Cox and Ray Berry (Group Scout Leader)

The new hall was dedicated by the Rector, Rev John Litton on 3rd March 1973 in the presence of the District Scout Commissioner, Mr Eric Tysoe, Jack Onslow Fane, and many representatives of the Oakley Scout and Guide Movement.

The premises soon became too small for the ever increasing number of children wishing to join all sections of the movement and parents, children, leaders and friends set about raising funds to build a far larger Headquarters at St John's Piece. Their efforts raised £16,000 towards the total cost of £62,000.

The balance was financed by generous grants from Hampshire County Council (£31,000) and Basingstoke and Deane Borough Council (£15,000). Alan Axford and Brian Purdue both from Oakley started work on the building on 20th March 1982, it was blessed during a service held by Canon John Litton and Deaconess Marjorie Honnor on 1st November 1982. Chief Scout Major–General Michael Walsh, officially opened the Headquarters on 19th March 1983. A further extension to the premises was opened at the Premises Committee Christmas Fair in 1993.

Blessing of the new Scout and Guide Headquarters at St Johns Piece on 1st November 1982
On stairs from left: Brian Busby, Wendy Wilson, Roger Wills, Marilyn Watkinson, Pam Moore, Helen Wills, Sarah Brown, Margaret Gould, Daphne Grace
Bottom row from left: Eric Moore (Group Scout Leader), Canon John Litton, Deaconess Marjorie Honnor, Pearl Richardson (District Guide Commissioner)

Other youth organisations: Over the years, various youth activities have been started and disbanded. 1921 saw the formation of the Lad's Club for boys who had left school and were under 18 years of age. In 1938, Drill and Dancing Classes were arranged for children of seven to ten.

In May 1973 the St Johns Youth Club re-opened, and on 6th November of the same year, the Toddlers Club was started, using the same premises. The Club later met at St Leonards Centre and spent many happy summer afternoons in The Rectory Gardens at the kind invitation of John and Helen Litton.

There is also a strong St Johns Ambulance Brigade unit which has just celebrated its tenth anniversary. Until July 1992 the unit met at Hilsea College, but following the school's closure they have transferred to East Oakley Village Hall, which is also the venue for the Wessex Rangers.

Sport, Song & Socials

Leisure Through The Years

Although 100 years ago working hours were long and hard, the men and women still appeared to find time and energy to take part in numerous activities. The enthusiasm continued through two world wars, the depression and many other social changes brought about by national events. Clubs were formed, some of which have now ceased to exist, whilst others remain today, further strengthened by the increase in population and wealth of the community.

In this chapter we look at a few leisure activities enjoyed by the inhabitants of the villages of Oakley, Deane, Newfound, Malshanger and East Oakley.

Oakley Football Club: According to a scrapbook of news–cuttings from the *Hants & Berks Gazette* kept by the late Mr F J Lee, there was a football club in existence in Oakley in 1921. The captain was R Sandom and matches were played at Clerken Green, near the Red Lion Inn . For several years the Club played in the Basingstoke Junior League and at one time ran two teams.

During the late 1920s there was no football club in the village although Oakley School had a boys team throughout this period.

Oakley School Football Team 1927/1928 Back row from left: Marcus Lee, Monty Hunt, Edwin Foote, Middle row from left: John Curtis, George Smith, Percy Gabb, William Moore, Ted Allen Front row from left: Alf Whitman, Jack Garrett, Arthur Dolton

A meeting was held in the early 1930s to try to revive football. The Club was reformed under the captaincy of Mr L Brooman and an application was made to use an area of ground near East Oakley Village Hall and to use the Hall as a changing room.

It is known that, at one stage, football was played next to George Smith's coalyard in Oakley Lane, where the monkey puzzle tree still grows. The youth team played in the field next to 'Salt Ash' in St Johns Road.

Just before the Second World War the Oakley team moved to Newfound Recreation Ground. They became known as Wootton St Lawrence FC and later went on to win the Basingstoke Junior Cup.

In 1967 an up and coming Chelsea FC star, Peter Houseman and his wife Sally moved to Oakley. It wasn't long before he had assessed the sad lack of football facilities for young boys in the village and, with the help of a number of fathers, got together a team to play friendly matches. He soon realised that a properly organised league for youngsters was necessary in the Basingstoke area. Under his guidance a number of Clubs were formed including Oakley Boys FC.

For their first 10 years the Club did not play a game in Oakley, with home games played either at Newfound Recreation Ground or Malshanger. In 1978 they moved into the new Peter Houseman Ground just off Rectory Road, which was named after the man who had contributed so much to football in the village before his tragic death in 1977.

Oakley Boys FC continues to thrive with teams from Under 9s to Under 15s. There are two senior teams for those players who can no longer be classed as 'boys'. In 1993 they celebrated 25 years of boys football by staging a two–day, six–a–side football tournament, inviting all the teams within the Peter Houseman league to take part.

It is understood that there was no senior Oakley FC team as such since just before the Second World War until the mid 1980s when the men's team was reformed and matches played again in the village.

Oakley Cricket Club: The earliest records of cricket in Oakley were of a match played against Basingstoke on a field next to the Red Lion Inn at Clerken Green on 23rd July 1835. Oakley lost by six wickets!

The Oakley Park Cricket Club was formed in 1854 by Lieut–Col Sir John Wallington of Oakley Hall after he had laid the playing table during the close season of 1853. Under his management the Club soon became one of the leading Clubs in this part of the country. Once a year there was a 'cricket week' at Oakley Park which used to attract spectators from far and wide.

Sport, Song And Socials: Leisure Through The Years

Oakley Cricket Club, circa 1910 with George Blewden, from Oakley Post Office (far right standing), Rev. Hume, the Rector of Oakley, (on left seated), Mr Peters, headmaster of Oakley School, (third row with beard), Alf Garrett (on his left), Bert Wyeth, local builder (fifth from left, third row), 'Ref' Garrett (left seated on ground)

Local matches were also played against teams from Hurstbourne Park, Hackwood Park, The Vyne & Basingstoke.

Very few records of the Club's cricket exist from towards the end of the last century up until the end of the First World War but it is known that the Club was in existence in 1910.

At the end of the First World War the Club came into its own again and during the 1920/21 season it only suffered one defeat. The team was captained by Mr Dollin who later had trials for Hampshire Cricket Club. At that time the pitch was still cut by a horse-drawn mower.

Canon Jeudwine became a member when appointed to the living of the village in 1919 and was Chairman and opening batsman for many of his years in Oakley.

Under the captaincy of Bill Collis and Leslie Lee the 1920s and 1930s were happy years for village cricket. At the end of the 1936 season it became obvious that the old wood–and–thatch pavilion, built in 1854, was unsafe. A new pavilion was purchased from Enham Village Centre at a cost of £136 and officially opened by Ellice Hicks Beach on 8th May 1937. At the same time the playing square was enlarged to permit a permanent fence and boundary. However, all the water had still to be drawn from the well at Keepers Cottage.

Sport, Song And Socials: Leisure Through The Years

Oakley Cricket Club in 1936 in front of the old pavilion
Standing from left: 'Ref' Garrett (umpire), R Kellow, C Hunt, Frank Neale, B Neale,
W Collis, J Bagley, J Garrett, G Wyeth, Bob Oliver (umpire)
Seated: G Eales, M Lee, L Lee (captain), F Neale, C Froome

Opening of the new pavilion on 8th May 1937. The match was against Sherborne St John. The season's tea ladies are standing at the front

During the Second World War very little cricket was played, but the late 1940s, the 1950s and early 1960s were perhaps the most successful times in the Club's history. The year 1950 appears to have been, particularly successful, for two players. On 29th May, playing against Heckfield, Marcus Lee scored the first century for Oakley and on 11th June, C Hunt took seven of the opponents wickets for eight runs.

In 1986 much-needed improvements were carried out to the 1937 pavilion to meet the requirements of the Hampshire Cricket League. These comprised the installation of electricity, changing rooms, showers, toilets and a bar! There was also the provision of a separate entrance so that players in their cricket whites did not need to negotiate a field full of cows to reach the square from the pavilion!

Today the Club continues to thrive at its ground in Oakley Park with a total of six adult and three junior teams playing midweek as well as weekends.

The 1952 Womens Institute scrapbook which was kindly lent to us states 'some years ago there was a Ladies Cricket Team' – but there is no indication of their success.

One or two snippets about another aspect of cricket – The Teas

Firstly, when the Club played at Clerken Green, Mr Few the landlord prepared the lunches and teas and his sons never missed a match on a Saturday.

Secondly, When Blewdens, and later Coopers & Field, supplied the cake it took the form of a lard cake – two feet long!

Oakley Tennis Club was formed about 1920 and members played at Sunbeam Cottage, then the home of Mrs Hume. Matches were played at Malshanger against teams from Whitchurch and Winchester. Later in the 1920s a court alongside Oakley Stores was also used.

By 1932 the Club was playing at Sunbeam Cottage and at Highlands, then owned by Mr Fookes. At their Annual General Meeting, held in the Parish Room on 30th November of that year, a scheme was proposed for public tennis courts and a site was decided upon between Mr Boon's Farm and Sunbeam Cottage on land owned by Mr F D Small. The estimated cost of the new courts including a pavilion, lawn mower, roller, nets, posts and wire was £22.15.0d (£22.75) and these were opened officially on 1st May 1933 by Brigadier General Sir Hill Child.

During the 1930s the Club held many dances and whist drives to raise funds to supplement the income from subscriptions of 7/6d (37.5p) and 5/– (25p) for juniors.

Sport, Song And Socials: Leisure Through The Years

The question of Sunday play was also raised at this time but Rev Jeudwine – a Vice–president – was opposed to this as the courts were on Glebe land.

In the late 1930s with the courts in poor condition, land at Pack Lane was leased for £2.5.0d pa and new courts were constructed. On 13th May 1939 a tournament was held on them.

With the outbreak of the Second World War the Club was closed, but in 1946 it had reformed, and was again looking for land for new courts. Permission was given by the School Managers for the use of the land forming part of the School Playing Field (now Beach Park) and one court was ready for play in June 1947.

Many successes were recorded throughout the 1950s and, in 1955, the present tennis club site was acquired on lease from Sir Jeremiah Colman. Two courts were prepared initially then on 17th October 1959, one hard court was opened by the Club's President, Lady Colman. The facility has since been increased to four hard courts.

Putting Club: This was formed on 16th December 1949 under the inspiring leadership of Sir Harold Gillies, the eminent plastic surgeon who lived at Yewbank in Rectory Road. The members worked hard to ensure the Putting Green on land adjoining the Barley Mow, was a very good one. It was thought in the early 1950s that it was the first and only Putting Club in the country.

It was officially opened on 22nd September 1950 by Mr Bernard Darwin, the President. Initially, there were twelve holes which were later increased to eighteen. During its lifetime the Club was very popular but it ceased in the late 1950s.

Official opening of the Putting Green on 22nd September 1950 From left: Bernard Darwin (President), Sir Jeremiah Colman, and Sir Harold Gillies (Vice Presidents)

Sport, Song And Socials: Leisure Through The Years

Brian Thornton's Silver Prize Accordion Band playing at Oakley Village Hall, Andover Road in the 1930s. Norman Cooper of Cooper & Field can be seen on the double bass

Badminton Club: The first record is of the formation of a club on 30th November 1951. The members played at courts marked out in the Village Hall at Andover Road. Whether this was the first club is not known. Badminton is still played at the Village Hall today but, with better facilities available in Basingstoke, many play there instead.

Bands: Before the Second World War there were two dance bands operating in the village. Firstly, Mr Seeney's band comprising Mr Bunn, the butcher, (saxophone), Mr Seeney from Beach Arms Service Station, (piano), Norman Cooper of Cooper & Field, (double bass), Mr Pipkin, the cobbler, (violin) and Laurie Brooman (drums/piano). The other, Brian Thornton's band from Basingstoke.

Later in the 1940s was a band, The Rythm Ramblers consisting of Cecil Edwards and Hazel Holloway (accordion), Paul Lucas (piano), Ray & Jerry Hale (accordion & drums) and Pat Woods (piano). All the bands were in demand for dances at East Oakley and Andover Road Villager Hall and also travelled to surrounding villages.

In the 1950s another band was started by fourteen year old Bob Wheeler who played the accordion. His eldest brother John played the drums, Harold Seeney the piano, George Pipkin the violin and Bertie Bunn played the saxophone. Their first engagement was at The Malshanger Club.

Sport, Song And Socials: Leisure Through The Years

East Oakley Village Hall formerly the Mens Club with library plaque on wall facing the road

Mothers' Union: The Oakley Mothers' Union branch was formed about 1900 with Mrs Hume, the wife of the then Rector as the first Enrolling Member. Her successor was a Mrs Milsom and later Mrs Jeudwine, the wife of the Canon Jeudwine. In 1934 she was obliged to give up this work due to the ill–health of her daughter. Mrs Bamford was then Enrolling Member until the Second World War when the office passed to Mrs Padfield, wife of the Rector at Wootton St Lawrence.

In 1942 the Oakley & Wootton St Lawrence branches joined together and the meetings were held alternatively in the Men's Club (now known as East Oakley Village Hall) and at Wootton St Lawrence, with a bus (probably one of Huntley's Buses) taking members to and fro. By 1950 Mrs Money, wife of a later vicar of Wootton St Lawrence was the Enrolling Member and there was a membership of 80.

At some point between the mid 1950s and the 1970s the Oakley and Wootton St Lawrence branch closed. On 20th November 1977 the Oakley branch was reformed but only lasted about thirteen years before it was again closed.

Libraries: The first library was started with books given by many people in the village and was situated in the Parish Room. Deane also had a library in Deane House Lodge which opened once a week.

In the early 1930s the Library was run under the Carnegie Trust through Hampshire County Council and in 1948 a fortnightly Mobile County Library was started at East Oakley. To this day, the County Council Library plaque remains on the front of East Oakley Village Hall.

It was noted in the Women's Institute scrapbook that in 1950 the librarians were Mrs Foote and Miss Light at Oakley Village Hall and Mrs Benson at East Oakley Village Hall, and they were Women's Institute members.

The two static libraries eventually closed to be replaced by twice–weekly visits by the Hampshire County Council Library Service Mobile Library van.

Sport, Song And Socials: Leisure Through The Years

Table Tennis Club: Oakley Ladies Ping Pong Club (later changed to Table Tennis Club) was started in 1929 at East Oakley Hall by kind permission of the Men's Club. Miss Boon was the first captain and the Club met and played matches on Saturday afternoons and evenings. In the early 1930s there were between 30 and 40 members.

In 1959 Ted Sherburn and Arthur Dolton started a Table Tennis Club in the Village Hall in Andover Road and games are still played there on Monday evenings.

Men's Club: Oakley Men's Club was in existence in 1914 and first met in the Reading Room but when it restarted in 1921 with Rev Jeudwine as Chairman, the club changed its venue. Members met on two evenings a week in what is now East Oakley Village Hall. All men from the age of eighteen were eligible as members.

During the period 1921–1941 the Men's Club gave the village probably the best social life of its history with high attendances at its whist drives and dances with bus loads coming from Basingstoke and neighbouring villages. The eagerly awaited 'Fur and Feather' Christmas Whist Drives were sold out (180 tickets) a month before the event.

Prizes at the 1929 event included three turkeys, two geese, four brace of pheasants, two ducks, two cockerels, four hens and three rabbits and a profit of £16.10s.0d was raised.

Club life consisted of billiards, cards, reading and music and in 1927 Sir Hill Child presented the Club with a magnificent full–size billiard table from Malshanger House.

The post war years of 1946–1950 were very difficult. Socials and dances were no longer held and the Club membership dwindled to such an extent that by the early 1950s it ceased to exist.

Malshanger Estate Social Club: The Club was formed in 1940 to provide social activities for the estate employees and their families. Club facilities included darts, table tennis, bar, monthly whist drives, shove–halfpenny and dominoes. There were also annual events such as parties for both children and adults, and a summer outing.

The Club closed during the Second World War and was used by the Army. It re–opened in 1962/63 and today, as Malshanger Sports & Social Club, still has sections for football, cricket, bowls, squash, darts and pool but membership is no longer restricted to estate employees.

Opening of Oakley Bowling Clubs' green at Malshanger in 1983. Photo shows Sir Michael & Lady Colman, Mrs Kay Kerley (President - Oakley Bowling Club) and the Presidents of Hampshire County Womens & Mens Bowling Associations

Sport, Song And Socials: Leisure Through The Years

Amateur Dramatic and Music Society: Not many people will know that Oakley once had a popular Amateur Dramatic and Music Society. Its inaugural concert was held in April 1931 and attracted 200 people. It was the idea of Mr E L Fitch, the village schoolmaster who was also produced the show. The opening song was sung by Rev Jeudwine. The Society continued to attract large audiences to its productions in the School Room during the 1930s.

Women's Institute: The Oakley and Deane Women's Institute was formed in 1918 by Mrs Walter of Malshanger House who was the first president. Between the two World Wars it flourished and members benefited greatly from the various lectures, demonstrations and social activities at the monthly meetings, held at first in the Reading Room and then, from 1938, the 'new' Village Hall in Andover Road.

During the Second World War petrol rationing brought an end to private transport to meetings and it became necessary to hire Mr Huntley's bus for this purpose.

Members were responsible for a great deal of jam making (something together with *'Jerusalem'* for which they are still remembered today) and some helped with the YMCA canteen for troops in Basingstoke.

Oakley & Deane Women's Institute 40th Birthday Party in April 1958 Mrs Hobbs (left) and Mrs Miles, both founder members are seen cutting the cake. The President in 1958, Mrs Nancy Kirby is in the centre foreground

Sport, Song And Socials: Leisure Through The Years

With the end of the war, Institute activities returned to normal, and it supported active drama and country dancing groups.

In 1992 Oakley & Deane Women's Institute celebrated 75 years of the movement in the village.

With the development of Oakley, membership increased from 50 to 120 by the Golden Jubilee in 1968. With membership at a maximum allowed at Andover Road Village Hall and an increasing waiting list, a second Women's Institute, the East Oakley Women's Institute was inaugurated in October 1969. Due to difficulties over a change from evening to afternoon meetings it was closed down in the mid 1970s.

In 1980 the Oakley Afternoon Women's Institute was formed with meetings held in the Methodist Church. These were later transferred to St Leonards Centre.

OAKLEY DRAMA SOCIETY PRESENTS
FRIENDS AND NEIGHBOURS
A Comedy by Austin Steele
FRI. & SAT., FEB. 20th & 21st
AT
OAKLEY VILLAGE HALL
(ANDOVER ROAD)
Tickets 6/- and 5/-
Obtainable from "Jean's", of Oakley Lane

A Beat Nite
with
MIKE STEVENS
and the
DOLPHINS
plus
THE ADDICTS
at
OAKLEY VILLAGE HALL
(Main Andover road)
SATURDAY,
AUGUST 29
3/6 at door
7.30 to 11 p.m.
Late Bus 11 p.m.

An advert from the Basingstoke Gazette August 1964

Carts and Carriages:

Transport Through The Century

Oakley Station looking towards Station Road, with staff on the platform, taken in 1900

The last 100 years has seen a tremendous change in modes of transport. People living in the village in 1894, whose main method of travel was either by foot, train or horse, could never have imagined that within 100 years the majority of the families would own a car and would think nothing of flying all over the world in aircraft that carried hundreds of people at a time. Even more incredible would have been the thought that several people would have actually travelled to and walked, on the moon. So, how has transport developed here in Oakley?

In 1894 Oakley Railway Station had already been built for 40 years. June 3rd 1854 saw the opening of the station and the line connecting Andover with Waterloo via Basingstoke. Three years later, the line was extended to Salisbury.

In 1914 the station staff consisted of Station Master, Booking Clerk, two signal men, and one porter. Passenger traffic was very heavy, particularly the workmen's train in the morning, as there was no other transport available to get to Basingstoke. Goods traffic was also very heavy and the goods yard was always busy. There were goods arriving for use in the village, such as coal for the coal merchants Phillips & Co who carried on a business at the station for many years, and local farms used the trains to transport hay, straw, and other crops.

Carts And Carriages: Transport Through The Century

A victim of the Beeching cuts, Oakley Station closed on 17th June 1963. Section 10 of the British Rail memorandum dated 9th July 1962, on the proposed closure, is of particular interest. It read :

'Possibility of Development:

The villages served by the station and the distances therefrom are:

Oakley (½ mile) East Oakley (1 mile)

Newfound (1 mile) Deane (1 ½ miles)

The combined population of these villages is approximately 750. A certain amount of housing development has taken place away from the station in the area of East Oakley but not in sufficient quantity to alter the traffic potential at Oakley Station.

The area is already served by frequent bus services connecting it with Basingstoke'.

This proved to be a short–sighted decision as by the mid 1970s, Oakley had developed to the size we know it today.

The other railway line which cuts through Oakley, the Waterloo to Southampton line was opened on 11th May 1840. In those days six trains a day connected Basingstoke with the capital and the maximum speed at which one would travel was 31 mph.

As there was no road transport when Oakley Cricket Club started using its grounds at Oakley Park in 1853, they used to stop the train opposite the pitch to allow the visiting teams to alight and scramble down the slight embankment.

A little way east of the bridge over Dummer Lane was the site of Wootton signal box, so called because when it was built it was within the Wootton Parish boundary.

Wootton Signal Box – showing Mr Parker the signalman

Battledown Flyover circa 1905, showing a train travelling from Southampton towards Basingstoke. St John's Copse and Breach Farm are in the background

Still further east towards Basingstoke, where the Southampton and Salisbury lines meet, is Battledown junction. It was built in 1897 and designed to be taken at 55 mph, is the only fly–over junction in Hampshire. Close by is Worting signal box.

An early example of the internal combustion engine seen around the village in the 1920s was the *Oakley Tulip* which belonged to Mr George Smith. The petrol–driven Maxwell engine and chassis were purchased by Mr Smith and Mr Sid Wyeth constructed the canopy to protect the passengers and driver. It used to be used for a variety of purposes; to take Oakley footballers and cricketers to matches, for day trips to Portsmouth and Bournemouth, to carry out a variety of haulage jobs and door to door delivery of the *Hants & Berks Gazette* (fore–runner to the *Basingstoke Gazette*) to name but a few. The *Oakley Tulip* was also used as a scavenger (*ie* rubbish) cart, the contents of which were tipped at Pardown near the strawberry fields.

Another, more modern, form of transport was Huntley's Buses. The business was started in the early 1930s by Mr Sidney Huntley who had been driving coaches and buses since the mid 1920s and had held a driving licence since 1910.

His first vehicle was like a Black Maria and seated twelve. He later acquired his 'Market Bus' in which he transported chicken and other produce from the village to Basingstoke market on a Wednesday morning. The buses (seven or eight at the height of the business) were based at first in a garage at the rear of 5 Oakley Lane the entrance to which was very much the same width as now. Later, they were kept at the Wheatsheaf at North Waltham.

Carts And Carriages: Transport Through The Century

The first service of the day left Pardown at 7.30 am to take workmen to Thorneycrofts and other places of employment in Basingstoke. There were no official bus stops and therefore, if one of the regulars was late, the driver would stop the bus at their door, the horn would be sounded and it would not proceed until the passenger was on board.

Competition from larger organisations finally forced the family to sell the business to Venture Limited, the fore–runner of the Hants and Dorset.

Of course, one final mode of transport must not be forgotten – the bicycle. It would appear that many people owned a bicycle, there was a Raleigh dealership at what is now Doltons Garage where bicycles could be bought and repairs carried out.

The 'Oakley Tulip' circa 1923 at the Southampton Agricultural Show
Back row from left: George Smith Snr, Jim Chant, (?), (?), (?), Mrs Wright (partly hidden), Jimmy Hale, Mrs Stratton, Polly Hale (with bag), Vi Dolton, Ernie Dolton, Mrs Dolton, Lizzie Hobbs (with basket)
Front row from left: (?), Arthur Hunt, Ruth Smith (small girl), Ada Smith, Tom Smith, George Smith Jnr.

Huntley's Coach

100

Carts And Carriages: Transport Through The Century

*Three ladies with bicycles outside Upper Farm (on the right) with the pond which was just past the present junction of The Drive and Hill Road.
(The photograph was taken looking towards the railway bridge)*

CAUTION CROSSING

One of the original Duck Signs erected by the Parish Council to remind motorists

Local Personalities

Over the last 100 years, Oakley has been home to a variety of eminent and interesting people. This chapter tells their story and that of one of two groups of people who play their part in the life of this area.

Sidney Eggars Bates: Although he lived at Manydown (in the Parish of Wootton St Lawrence), Mr Bates owned much of the land at East Oakley and Pardown and gave the village the ground on which St Johns Church and St Johns Youth Centre now stand. The family also gave the area known as Newfound Recreation Ground to Wootton Parish Council to provide sports facilities for the area. It was agreed in 1993 that Oakley & Deane Parish Council would lease and maintain the land, thus preserving the area for the use of the whole village.

Sidney Bates was a member of the ship–owners Edward Bates & Sons of Liverpool and his descendants still farm the various farms that form the Manydown Company.

William Wither Bramston Beach lived in the village during the whole of his life. Born on Christmas Day 1826, the Oakley Hall estate passed to him on his father's death on 22nd November 1856. He was educated at Eton and Christ Church College, Oxford and gained a BA in 1849 and later an MA. He was a JP, a Captain in the Hampshire Yeomanry Cavalry and became the Provincial Grand Master of Freemasons of Hampshire and the Isle of Wight.

In addition, William Beach had a distinguished political career as a Member of Parliament for Hampshire for 44 years and a Privy Councillor. At the time of his death at Westminster Hospital, after a riding accident on 3rd August 1901, he was Father of the House of Commons.

On 8th October 1857, he married Caroline Chichester on 8th October 1857 who became one of the Oakley School Managers. She took a great interest in the running of the school which her father–in–law had built in the early 1850s. She died on 29th March 1918. They had three children, Archibald William Hicks Beach, Ellice Michael Hicks Beach and Alice Margaret Beach.

In this the centenary year of the Parish Council, William Wither Bramston Beach will be remembered primarily as Oakley's first Parish Council Chairman. He is buried at Deane.

Ellice Hicks Beach was the younger son of W W B Beach. During his life he became the Chairman of Magistrates, and was second Secretary at the British Embassy in Moscow. Following in his parents footsteps, he took a great interest in the local schools, and became great friends with Mr Ellis–Jones and Mr and Mrs Platt of Hilsea College. He used to visit them for tea every Thursday. He was also a regular visitor at Oakley School. He remained a bachelor, and for many years until his death in September 1948, he lived at Deane Manor.

Local Personalities

Miss Harriet Jeannie Blackburn lived in Oakley all her life and taught the infants at Oakley School for some 42 years. Mrs Wilson of St Johns Piece recollects both her mother, herself and her children were all taught by Miss Blackburn. In addition to teaching, Miss Blackburn was the organist at St Johns Church for many years and a member of the choir at St Leonards. She was also a member of a very successful concert party while Mr Ridges was headmaster at the school.

A memorial to Jeannie Blackburn was erected on the lawn at the old school and later moved to its present site at the Junior School. It took the form of a bird table, designed and constructed by Mr Sharpe and financed from donations made by her many friends. It was unveiled by Mr Ellice Hicks Beach on 29th May 1946, on the anniversary of the day Miss Blackburn began teaching at the school in 1902.

Dr Robert Gallimore was the village's first resident doctor, moving to the village and starting his surgery at Mitchells, Hill Road in 1932. He retired after 35 years of service to the community (which had expanded and changed considerably) in 1967. He was very much liked by his patients who presented him with an inscribed silver bowl and a cheque for about £300. In addition to being a GP he was also the surgeon who removed the then young Alan Hunt's tonsils on the kitchen table at the Hunt's home, a tin bungalow in Oakley Lane. During his time in Oakley he married the District Nurse and they had two sons.

Teachers at Oakley School in 1910
Top row from left: Miss Blackburn, Miss Phillips, Miss Kneller
Bottom row from left: Miss Winterton, Mr Peters (Headmaster)

Local Personalities

Dr Robert Gallimore (right) being presented with his retirement gift from his patients in Oakley and the surrounding district, by Col R M Bamford

Sir Harold Gillies lived at Yewbank for a number of years in the 1940s and 1950s. He was an eminent plastic surgeon developing many new techniques during World War II when he was in charge of the work at Rooksdown. He became known as the 'Founding Father of Plastic Surgery'. There are still men alive today who were badly burned or wounded during the war, who owe their present quality of life to his skill. In his spare time, he enjoyed painting and often visited Hilsea College to paint in the grounds. Another interest was golf. Sir Harold was the inspiration for, and one of the founder members of, the Putting Club whose green was built next to the Barley Mow in the early 1950s.

Peter Houseman was one of a large family brought up in Battersea. In 1966 he married Sally, a young lady from Cirencester, whom he had met when he was about thirteen years old. They lived at Severn Gardens in Oakley.

Peter was a footballer in the Chelsea team when they won the FA Cup, and he used his skill and dedication to the game to help many youngsters in Oakley, during the nine years the family lived here. He formed the Basingstoke Under 15 league and became their President with his wife Sally acting as Secretary. In addition, he trained the Oakley boys who with his great encouragement won the Cup and the league.

After Peter was transferred to Oxford, the family, including by then their three sons, decided to move. In the early hours of Mothering Sunday in 1977, on their return from a charity function, both he and Sally together with two new friends, were killed in an horrific road accident.

Local Personalities

Peter Houseman with the Oakley Boys Football Team
Back row from left: Julian Butler, Anthony Goodall, Gary Walters, (?), Neil Jolley, David Buckland, Ainsley Norman, Nick Aylward, Andy Hugman, Paul Gleed, Colin Jolley, (?)
Front row from left: David Fiske, Bobby Upton, (?), Simon Blair, Andrew Terry, Andy Gleed, Neil Godley. Graham Brown, (?), Andrew Green

He will be remembered for many years by the youngsters who were trained by him and his name will live on in Oakley through the recreation ground just off Rectory Road which was named after him.

Canon George Herbert Jeudwine was inducted as Rector of St Leonards, Church Oakley by the Archdeacon of Winchester on 3rd May 1919. He was ordained at Manchester Cathedral on 29th September 1907, became Director of Religious Education for the Diocese of Winchester on 1st November 1933 and an Honorary Canon of Winchester in 1941.

He was made a Parish Councillor in November 1922 and served a total of 38 years. He became Chairman in April 1931 and retired from the post in May 1960 when, it is believed, he moved away from the village.

Local Personalities

Canon G H Jeudwine, Rector of Oakley 1919 to 1960

His first wife Beatrice Mary, who had been instrumental in the formation of a Girl Guide Company in July 1922, died on 19th July 1954. Her ashes were buried in St Leonards Churchyard. Canon Jeudwine married Mary Pelham Browne on 30th September 1955.

Canon John Champernowne Litton was born in Hampshire in 1924 and educated at Eton, Oxford and Lincoln Theological College. He also followed courses of study for the Army and for the Malayan Civil Service. After serving as a Curate in Cannock, Staffordshire, and Rector of Rockbourne in Hampshire he was inducted as Rector of Oakley on 3rd August 1972 by the Bishop of Southampton. During his twelve-year ministry in the village, both he and his wife Helen worked tirelessly, becoming involved in many aspects of life in Oakley.

He took a great interest in the Scout and Guide movements, was a school governor for many years, and was the founder of the secular Community Care Organisation which still continues to help those in need after nearly 20 years.

He will be remembered by the many families who moved to the village in the 1970s for the welcome he gave them, whether they were churchgoers or not. Many people will remember him riding around the village on his bicycle – particularly between St Leonards and The Rectory. John Litton died of cancer in October 1984.

Rev F S H Marle was Rector of Deane during the war years and into the 1950s. During the Second World War he was Deane's Air Raid Warden and, with Ellice Hicks Beach, planned the Church Fêtes, for many years, held at Hilsea College.

Nurses: During our research older residents related various tales about the Nurses who have cared for the sick in the village over the years. Once such tale was about Nurse Wyeth who lived in The Thatched Cottage, in the grounds of The Manor. Before she left on her bicycle to do her rounds, she would put a message in her window describing her route so that, if anyone needed her in an emergency, she could be easily found.

For thirty one years between 1931 and 1962 Oakley, and much of the surrounding district, was ably cared for by Nurses Witts and Jays. They first met when they were both pursuing their careers in Wolverhampton, the town where Nurse Witts had started her training back in 1929. In 1931 they both moved to Ashe Close at Wootton St Lawrence which consisted of three cottages, one to provide accommodation for the Nurses and the other two for old age pensioners on whom they could keep an eye. In all, over six hundred people contributed to their retirement present in 1962. Nurse Witts, who died some years ago, will also be remembered as the founder of the Good Companions in 1957.

Jack Onslow Fane: Mr and Mrs Jack Onslow Fane came to live at Oakley Manor in 1938. They moved to Oakley Hall in 1939 and thereafter to Steventon. At the outbreak of the Second World War in 1939 Mr Onslow Fane joined the Royal Air Force, first as a Flight Lieutenant in the Balloon Defence Corps, and later in Flying Training Command. After the war they moved to Candover Park, returning to Oakley and East Oakley House in the early 1950s.

His chief interest was in boxing and in 1931 Jack had become the Boxing Board of Control's youngest administrative steward. He went on to be elected vice–president in 1946, permanent chairman in 1949 and president in 1950. He was also a patron of all field sports and a keen shot.

Whilst in Oakley he became associated with the Conservatives, the Scouts and the Cricket and Tennis Clubs. He died on 5th February 1984 at the age of 83.

Policemen: There has been a village 'bobby in Oakley since before the turn of the century, when he and his family lived at 1 Hill Road. It is believed that PC501 Stuart Hall was the last policeman to live at that address.

Police records for Oakley village can only be traced back to 1935 when the total population of Oakley, Deane and Wootton St Lawrence, which made up the Oakley beat, was 1,572. The records kept by the police were exhaustive at that time and included such things as holders of Firearm Certificates, Shotgun Certificates and provisional driving licences. There were also records of registered Aliens, of which there were several among the students of Hilsea College. A policeman would also have among his records a list of persons who kept a motor car, which he would be permitted to use for Police purposes.

Records were also maintained of farmers who kept livestock and working dogs. In addition to what would be a policeman's normal duties, he was also a Diseases of Animal Inspector, responsible for the issue of animal movement licences, the inspection of slaughter houses and supervision of sheep–dipping etc. During any outbreaks of diseases such as Foot and Mouth, or Swine Fever, the local policeman was responsible for arranging for the destruction of the carcasses and only relinquished these responsibilities to the Ministry of Agriculture in 1980.

Canon John Litton – well known in the village for cycling in his clerical robes

Local Personalities

Rev F H S Marle, his wife and Mr Ellis–Jones (founder of Hilsea College) at Deane Church Fête held in the college grounds

Before the advent of modern technology the local Police Officer would have to cycle daily to Basingstoke Police Station, then in Mark Lane, for his supervision and correspondence. He would also have to make regular contact or 'points' with his supervising Sergeant, usually from a public telephone box around midnight, to check his welfare and notebook and to discuss any problems.

The first occupant of the new Police House in Oakley Lane, on 22nd March 1968, was PC744 John Pimblett. In 1976 PC532 Dave Bellchamber was transferred to Oakley from Havant and became well known by old and new residents alike. Although he was transferred to Basingstoke in 1987 he continued to live in Oakley until his death while still serving in the Hampshire Constabulary in January 1993. Our present village policeman, PC1962 Brian Oliver, came to Oakley in January 1986.

The role of the Police Officer in the community remains unchanged and he is still responsible for the protection of life and property, the prevention and detection of crime, and the prosecution of offenders against the Peace. He remains an ordinary citizen, but given additional powers by the issue of the Queen's Warrant.

Brigadier Henry (Dick) Vernon retired to Oakley in 1970 after a career in the Army spanning more than 30 years. In 1937 he joined the 60th Rifle Regiment spending a lot of time abroad. Following his retirement, he spent six years as Honorary Colonel of the 39 Signal Regiment, Territorial Army and has served on the Oakley and Deane Parish Council for the Church Oakley Ward. However, his chief interest is his work with schools and young people.

In recognition of his public duties and fine Army career, in August 1984, he had the honour of being appointed a Deputy Lieutenant of Hampshire. This position is for life and his duties are to represent the Lord Lieutenant (the recently–appointed Mrs Mary Fagan who also lives in the Parish, at Deane) at functions in the County when he may appear in his Army uniform.

Prologue –

A Future From The Past

At the beginning of this book we described life in Church and East Oakley, Deane and Newfound as it probably was in 1894 and, in the ensuing pages we have tried, and hopefully succeeded, to provide an insight into the people and events contributing to the life of the village during the last 100 years.

In this last chapter we compare 1894 with 1994 and look to the future.

Although the main road structure has changed little since 1894, many side roads and housing estates have been constructed during the last 30 years on land which was previously used for agriculture. Whereas the population of Deane has decreased from 121 in 1891 to 88 in the 1991 Census, the population of what is now generally known as Oakley and Newfound has increased nearly tenfold from approximately to 5,843 in the same period. It is however interesting to note that there has been no equivalent increase in the number of Parish Councillors.

In 1894 the majority of the children were taught in the two rooms which now form part of St Leonards Centre. At present, there are three play schools for the pre–school children, an Infants School and Junior School in the centre of the village and in excess of 450 of our eleven to sixteen year–olds travel to various schools in the area for their secondary education. In addition, many of the school–leavers continue their education at the local sixth–form colleges and farther afield at university, something unheard of in 1894.

Travel is certainly far easier than 100 years ago but many people living in Oakley today must wish that Dr Beeching had communicated with the planners and thus not 'axed' Oakley Railway Station!

Shopping habits have of course changed over the years. Local village shops have suffered with the emergence of the local Superstores and the availability of more exotic stock. However, although the number of shops has decreased over the years, Oakley has retained the most important ones that provide a valuable service to the community.

Youth and leisure organisations have come and some have gone, however even with the many attractions available in Basingstoke, the village can still boast a large number of clubs and leisure pursuits for all age groups.

What of the future?

In June of this year the Parish Council agreed that a Youth Parish Council for eleven to eighteen year–olds should be formed to provide them with an opportunity to make a contribution to the future of their village. By the time this book is published, elections will have been held and the Youth Parish Councillors will have started on their first project.

Prologue— A Future From The Past

At the other end of the scale, we still have to wait until next year to hear the final decision of the Local Government Commission into the future of Hampshire County Council and whether we go into the next 100 years of the Parish Council movement with one tier of the system removed.

1994 has been the year in which Mrs Roz Phillips and Mr Gerry Burnell (the head teachers of the Infant School and Junior School respectively) have retired after many years of service to the young children of the village. Therefore with the appointment of two new Headmistresses, 1995 will mark the beginning of a new chapter in the life of both schools.

1995 is election year for the Parish Council and in May all the Councillors retire, some permanently but others will seek re-election to the Council for another term of four years.

Although the village has grown since 1894, parts of it now being unrecognisable, from reading through the Minute Books for the last 100 years we still deal with many of the same problems as our predecessors – street lighting, recreation facilities, allotments etc.

A final thought – since the 1970s what is known by many as the 'Village Envelope' has been in force. This is a line drawn around the village outside of which new building is not permitted. The purpose of this is to protect the green 'gap' between Oakley and Basingstoke. With the need for more new houses, our 'village envelope' is constantly being threatened. If these protective measures fail, there will be no village of Oakley, no 'Oakley – The Last 100 Years' in 2094 and no bi-centennial celebrations of its Parish Council.

Rectory road pond and Blewdens delivery cart

List of Photographs

All Saints Church, Deane
Bakers of Oakley – coal lorry
Barley Mow (The), Oakley Lane
Battledown Flyover
Beach Arms Garage
Beech Lane
Bowling Club
Brian Thornton's Silver Prize Accordion Band
Brownies – 1957/58
Bulls Bushes Farm
Carnival Princess – Coronation celebrations, 1953
Claypits
Croft (The), Hill Road – Smith's Coalyard,
Deane Gate Inn, Deane
Deane Hill House
Deane showing flooding
Deepwell Cottage, Oakley Lane
Diocesan Missionary Pageant (1931)
Doltons Garage
East Oakley House
Ebeneezer Cottage, Hill Road
Fancy Dress Football Team (1937 Coronation)
Firs (The), St Johns Road
Fox Inn, Newfound
Gallimore (Dr Robert)
Garrett (T) – Shoeing Smith, Oakley Lane
Garrett family wedding, circa 1902
Garrett's (T & J) Yard, Oakley Lane
Girl Guides at camp, circa 1920
Girl Guides Pantomime (1978)
Group of Boys (circa 1915)
Hill Road – showing Police House,
Home Guard in uniform
Huntleys Bus
Jeudwine (Canon)
Ladies on Bicycles, Hill Road
Ladies and Children at Oakley Hall
Litton (Canon John)
Malborough Villas, Oakley Lane
Malshanger House, circa 1909
Marle (Rev.) – Vicar of Deane
Mears Garage, Newfound

List of Photographs

Mount (The), Hill Road
Newfound Weslyan Methodist Chapel
Oakley Cricket Club, circa 1910
Oakley School – Infants in 1910
Oakley School – Older children in 1910
Oakley School – Teachers in 1910
Oakley School early 1900s
Oakley School – after 1924
South View, Oakley Lane circa 1910
'Oakley Tulip'
Oakley Cricket Club – New Pavilion – 1937
Oakley Hall – North front from the air
Oakley & Deane Womens Institute's 40th birthday party
Oakley Cricket Club – Old Pavilion, – 1936
Oakley School Country Dancers, circa 1928
Oakley Manor
Oakley Boy Scouts soon after formation
Oakley School Boys Football Team
Old cottages behind Oakley School, circa 1902
Old Poor Houses, Newfound
Onslow Fane Hall – official opening
Parade outside Methodist Chapel
Peter Houseman
Peter Gannon – well digging
Pond and Forge Cottage, Oakley Lane
Pond, East Oakley with horses drinking
Pond, East Oakley – after snow storm 1908
Post Office, Church Oakley (Blewdens)
Post Office, Rectory Road (Cooper and Field)
Putting Green, Oakley Lane
Railway Cottages, Hill Road
Railway Station
Railway Terrace, Hill Road
Rectory Road Pond and Blewdens Delivery Cart
Red Lion Inn, Clerken Green
Scout Headquarters – Blessing the new building
St Johns Piece
St Johns Church, East Oakley
St Leonards Church, Church Oakley
Street Party for the Silver Jubilee in 1977
Sunbeam Cottage – School Room
Upper Farm Farmhouse
Wootton Signal Box